Grammar Sense

WORKBOOK 2

Angela Blackwell

OXFORD

UNIVERSITY PRESS

198 Madison Avenue
New York, NY 10016 USA

Great Clarendon Street
Oxford OX2 6DP England

Oxford   New York
Auckland   Bangkok   Buenos Aires   Cape Town   Chennai
Dar es Salaam   Delhi   Hong Kong   Istanbul   Karachi   Kolkata
Kuala Lumpur   Madrid   Melbourne   Mexico City   Mumbai
Nairobi   São Paulo   Shanghai   Taipei   Tokyo   Toronto

OXFORD is a trademark of Oxford University Press.

ISBN 0-19-436621-9

Editorial Manager: Janet Aitchison
Editorial Development, Project Management,
    and Production: Marblehead House, Inc.
Production Manager: Shanta Persaud
Production Controller: Zainaltu Jawat Ali

Illustrations: Roger Penwill, Seitu Hayden
Cover Design: Lee Ann Dollison
Cover Photo: Kevin Schafer / Peter Arnold, Inc.

The authors and publisher are grateful for permission to reprint the following photographs:

p. 1, ©PhotoDisc; **p. 19**: ©Retna Ltd. USA; **p. 72**: ©PhotoDisc; **p. 84**: ©The Museum of Modern Art/Licensed by SCALA/Art Resource, NY; **p. 109**: ©PhotoDisc; **p. 116**: ©PhotoDisc.

The authors and publisher are grateful for permission to reprint the following text excerpts:

p. 12: from "Leaving on a Jet Plane," © Cherry Lane Music. Reprinted with permission; **p. 17:** from *A-Z Encyclopedia of Jokes*, © Parade Publications; **p. 19:** from "Robin Williams: Finding His Way Back," © Readers Digest (UK Edition), March, 1999; **p. 30:** from "Some Will Go the Extra Mile," © Copy Right Clearance Center Inc. Reprinted with permission; **p. 60:** from "Weird and Wonderful Hobbies," © Waldman Publishing. Reprinted with permission; **p. 104:** from "Rich in Cash, But Not in Happiness," © San Francisco Chronicle. Reprinted by permission; **p. 122:** from "Happy Birthday," © Waldman Publishing.

Every effort has been made to trace and secure permission for all copyright material. In the event of any oversight or omission, we would appreciate any information that would enable us to do so.

Printing (last digit): 10 9 8 7 6 5 4 3 2 1

Printed in Hong Kong

Special thanks to the following students for permission to print their work:
Patty Chow, Mandy Huang, Ryan Chiu

Contents

1 The Simple Present

FORM

1 Examining Form

Read this letter and complete the tasks below.

Dear Emily
By Emily Fields

Dear Emily,

My husband and I <u>are</u> very happy. He helps me with the housework, doesn't complain, and
5 always remembers my birthday. He is kind and honest. My husband loves me, and I love him.

But I have a problem: My husband doesn't talk to me very
10 much. He goes to work, and when he comes home in the evening, he watches TV. Sometimes he talks to me during the programs, but usually he just sits in silence. I
15 don't know why. He isn't angry at me. He just doesn't seem interested in talking.

I don't go out to work, so I don't have many friends and
20 sometimes I need to talk. But my husband doesn't understand this. What advice do you have?

—*Bored in Birmingham*

1. There are many verbs in the letter. The first one is underlined. Underline six more.

2. What tense does the writer use in the letter? _____

Complete this text with the simple present form of the verbs in parentheses.

Does your family eat dinner together? Many families don't. A group of high school students was interviewed about what happens at dinnertime in their homes. Here are the results:

Only about half of the students __eat__ (eat) dinner with other family
₁

members. These teenagers _____ (enjoy) dinnertime and _____
₂ ₃

(see) it as a time to relax and talk.

One boy _____ (talk) to his mother while he is eating, but they often
₄

_____ (argue). And some families _____ (not talk) much
₅ ₆

during dinner. They _____ (watch) television while they are eating.
₇

One girl _____ (fix) her own dinner and _____ (eat) it
₈ ₉

alone. This is often because her parents _____ (not get) home in time to
₁₀

eat dinner with her.

Read what Lee says about her English skills and complete the task below.

> I don't speak English at home because my parents speak
> only Chinese. But I speak English at work and with some
> friends. Sometimes my friends correct my pronunciation. I
> don't mind that; I think it helps me.
> My listening skills are pretty good. I listen to songs
> in English. I watch movies in English, too. My brother
> watches them with me.
> Reading and writing are more difficult for me. I don't
> read English very often, and I almost never write it. I
> think my writing has a lot of grammar mistakes, but maybe I
> worry too much.

Rewrite Lee's text in the third person (*she*). Change pronouns and the form of the verbs. Do not change anything else.

   Lee doesn't speak English at home because her parents speak only

Chinese. But she . . . .

_____

_____

_____

_____

A. Complete these questions with *Do, Does, Is,* or *Are.*

1. _Do_____ you like the musicians?

2. _____ you from around here?

3. _____ you like this club?

4. _____ you here with friends, or are you alone?

5. _____ your friend have blond hair and glasses?

6. _____ that her over there?

7. _____ she Armenian, too?

8. _____ she speak English?

B. Match the questions in part A with these answers.

_4_ **a.** I'm with a friend.

____ **b.** No, she isn't. She's Russian.

____ **c.** No. I'm from Armenia.

____ **d.** No, she doesn't. She has dark hair.

____ **e.** Yes, it is.

____ **f.** Just a little.

____ **g.** Yeah. They're OK.

____ **h.** Yes. It's great.

Read these facts about the United States and complete the task below.

U.S. FACTS

1. Most Americans live near cities.

2. Most people go to work by car.

3. Very few people (five percent) use public transportation to go to work.

4. Most people retire at age 65.

5. Most families have two or more televisions.

6. Many people study at a college or university after high school.

7. Most Americans move every five years.

8. Most American women marry at age 25.

Write information questions for the answers.

1. Where _do most Americans live?_ _____

   Near cities.

2. How _____

   By car.

3. How many _____

   Very few people. Only five percent.

4. When _____

   At age 65.

5. How many _____

   Two or more.

6. What _____

   They study at a college or university.

7. How often _____

   Every five years.

8. When _____

   At age 25.

MEANING AND USE

6 **Understanding the Simple Present**

A. Read the paragraphs below. Where does each one come from? Write the letter of the appropriate source next to each paragraph.

SOURCES	
a. advertisement	**d.** biology textbook
b. computer manual	**e.** article from a magazine for parents
c. personal letter	**f.** magazine interview with an athlete

___d___ **1.** All South American monkeys live in trees, and they eat mostly leaves, fruit, and insects. Some African and Asian monkeys spend most of their lives on the ground and eat many different kinds of foods.

_____ **2.** During the baseball season, I always do things a certain way. If I eat some chicken before a game and we win the game, then I eat chicken before every game. After the games, I eat brownies with ice cream.

_____ **3.** Our fruitcake is a great holiday gift for family or friends. It tastes delicious. Everyone loves it. And it costs only $6.99!

_____ **4.** Let's start with some important terms. The *desktop* is what you see on the screen (if you don't have programs on the screen). The desktop has icons. *Icons* are small pictures on your desktop. They represent programs.

_____ **5.** This semester, I have four classes in a row on Mondays, Wednesdays, and Fridays (including one at 8:00 A.M. YUCK!), but Tuesdays and Thursdays I sleep late. I work in the restaurant two nights a week.

_____ **6.** In many families, children help with chores like making beds and doing dishes. Chores teach kids about responsibility and the importance of work. Kids complain about their chores, but they feel better when they do them. Chores make kids an active part of the family.

B. Look back at the paragraphs in part A. Which paragraph uses the simple present to:

___6___ **a.** talk about general truths?

_____ **b.** tell about scientific facts?

_____ **c.** tell about scheduled events?

_____ **d.** describe a person's habits and routines?

_____ **e.** give definitions?

_____ **f.** talk about states (likes, taste, etc.), not actions?

COMBINING FORM, MEANING, AND USE

7 Editing

There are eight errors in this student's composition. The first one has been corrected. Find and correct seven more.

My country ~~have~~ _has_ a tropical climate. The two seasons is summer and winter. Summer go from April to October. In summer it gets very hot. The temperature sometimes reach 40° Celsius. It also rain a lot in summer. Winter in my country begin in November. In winter, it is cooler, and it not rain very much. I like the weather better in the winter because I no like hot weather.

8 Writing

Follow the steps below to write a descriptive paragraph.

1. Think about your routines for Saturday (or for another day of the week). Write a list of the things you usually do on that day.

   Here's an example:

   On Saturday I usually . . .

   - get up at 9:00 A.M.
   - do things around the house
   - work in the garden
   - work on my car
   - repair things
   - have dinner with friends

2. On a separate sheet of paper, write a paragraph describing your routines for the day you chose. Use your notes, and put your activities in the correct time order. Use the simple present.

   On Saturday I usually get up at 9:00 A.M. Then I do things around the house. In the morning, I work in the garden. I rake the leaves and mow the lawn. In the afternoon, I work on my car or repair things. . . .

2 Imperatives

FORM

Read this brochure from a car rental company and complete the tasks below.

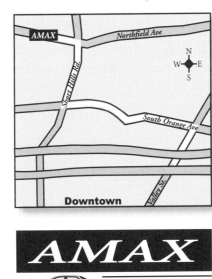

To get to AMAX Car Rental from downtown:
- <u>Drive</u> north on Valley Street.
- Go through two traffic lights.
5 - Turn left onto South Orange Avenue at the third traffic light.
- Stay on South Orange for four miles.
- Make a right onto Short Hills Road.
- Drive for two miles.
10 - Turn left onto Northfield Avenue. AMAX is #228 on the right.

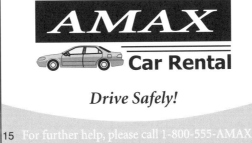

Drive Safely!

15 For further help, please call 1-800-555-AMAX

1. There are nine examples of imperatives in the brochure. The first one is underlined. Underline eight more.

2. Does an imperative sentence have a subject? _____

Rewrite these sentences as commands. Use imperatives. You do not have to use all the words.

1. You should turn on the engine.

   Turn on the engine.

2. You need to let go of the hand brake.

   _____

3. You should put the car into drive.

   _____

4. You should check the rearview mirror.

   _____

5. You need to turn the steering wheel to the right.

   _____

6. You shouldn't go so fast.

   _____

3 **Working on Affirmative and Negative Imperatives**

Use the verbs below to complete the information about what to do in an earthquake. Write affirmative or negative imperative sentences, using capital letters where necessary.

check	know	have

Before an earthquake, _check_ your house for items that may fall down.
Always _____ a week's supply of food and water in the house.
_____ where to meet your family if an emergency happens.

go	panic	go

During a quake, _____. If you are indoors, _____ outdoors:
It is more dangerous outdoors. If you are outdoors, _____ to an open area.

move	check	use

After a quake, when the shaking stops, _____ for injuries. If a person has
serious injuries, _____ that person; instead, wait for help. If everyone is OK
and you leave the building, _____ the elevator to leave. Stairs are safer.

MEANING AND USE

Match the signs to the places.

_e_ **1.** Please wait for the next available teller.

_____ **2.** Exit here in an emergency.

_____ **3.** In case of fire, use stairs for exit. Do not use elevator.

_____ **4.** Keep all medicines out of the reach of children.

_____ **5.** Open this end.

_____ **6.** Please wait to be seated.

_____ **7.** Do not feed the animals.

_____ **8.** Do not disturb.

a. On a door that leads outside a building

b. In a restaurant

c. On a bottle of aspirin

d. On a box

e. In a bank

f. In a zoo

g. On the door of a hotel room

h. Next to an elevator

5 **Giving Advice**

Complete these tips for air travelers. Use the imperative form of one of the verbs below.

arrive	bring	call	check	chew	drink	enjoy	fasten	listen	remove

1. _Call_ the airline a day in advance to confirm your flight.

2. _____ the departure time before leaving home.

3. _____ at the airport at least two hours before your flight.

4. _____ your ticket and at least one form of identification.

5. _____ sharp objects from your hand luggage.

6. On the plane, _____ to the safety announcements.

7. _____ your seat belt.

8. In flight, _____ a lot of water.

9. _____ gum during take-off or landing.

10. _____ your flight!

Match the sentences in the box to the pictures below. Then look again at each picture and circle the correct use of each imperative.

Get up!	Have a seat.	Let me see, please.
Look out!	Don't worry about it.	Hurry up!

1. <u>Hurry up!</u>

request   directions   (command)

4. _____

directions   warning   offer

2. _____

offer   warning   request

5. _____

offer   command   directions

3. _____

advice   offer   request

6. _____

offer   warning   request

COMBINING FORM, MEANING, AND USE

Write directions from your house to each of the places below. Use the affirmative and negative imperatives and the expressions in the box when possible.

turn right	turn left	go to the corner	don't go past	follow

1. your school

   Walk one block and turn right at May Street.

2. your friend's house

   _____

3. the post office

   _____

4. the bus stop

   _____

On a separate sheet of paper, write a paragraph in which you give advice to a friend. He or she is moving from a small town to a large city to study. Give your friend advice on some or all of the topics below. Use affirmative and negative imperatives.

using public transportation	meeting new people
walking on the street at night	finding a place to live
keeping valuables (money, credit cards, jewelry, etc.) safe	finding a part-time job
	buying groceries

When you move to _____ , don't walk alone on the street late at night. Don't carry a lot of money or wear a lot of jewelry. . . .

3 The Present Continuous

FORM

1 Examining Form

"Leaving on a Jet Plane" is a classic song from the 1970s. Read this excerpt from the song and complete the tasks below.

Leaving on a Jet Plane

All my bags are packed, and I'm ready to go
I'm standing here outside your door
I hate to wake you up to say goodbye
5 *But the dawn is breaking, it's early morn*
The taxi's waiting, he's blowing his horn
Already I'm so lonesome I could die
So kiss me and smile for me
Tell me that you'll wait for me
10 *Hold me like you'll never let me go*
'Cause I'm leaving on a jet plane
Don't know when I'll be back again
Oh babe, I hate to go

1. There are five examples of the present continuous in the song. The first one is underlined. Underline four more.

2. How is the present continuous formed? _____

Complete the paragraph with the present continuous form of the verbs in parentheses. Use contractions when possible.

Right now, I <u>'m standing</u> in the living room, and I
1

_____ (look) out the window. It is a beautiful day, and the sun
2

_____ (shine). My three boys are in the front yard. They
3

_____ (play) with a garden hose. They _____
4   5

(wear) their new clothes, but they _____ (not/think) about that.
6

They _____ (have) a wonderful time. My oldest boy
7

_____ (spray) the two younger ones with the hose. They
8

_____ (not/run) away. They _____ (try) to get
9   10

the hose away from him, and he _____ (not/let) them get the hose.
11

My wife _____ (tell) him to stop, but he _____
12   13

(not/pay) attention. The two younger boys _____ (laugh). They
14

_____ (get) very wet!
15

Writing Information Questions

Write information questions about the underlined words and phrases below.

1. You're going <u>somewhere</u>.

   <u>Where are you going?</u>

2. Your friends are traveling <u>somehow</u>.

   _____

3. The boss is talking to <u>someone</u>.

   _____

4. That child is crying <u>for some reason</u>.

   _____

5. Susan and John are going <u>somewhere</u>.

   _____

6. <u>Someone</u> is following us.

   _____

MEANING AND USE

4 **Contrasting Routines with Activities in Progress**

Complete these sentences with *it rains* or *it's raining*.

1. <u>It rains</u> _____ here every night.

2. Oh, no! _____.

3. _____ a lot in January, but it doesn't snow.

4. I don't want to go out because _____.

5. The weather is terrible in November. _____, and it's very windy.

6. Let's wait here a while longer. I think _____.

7. _____ every winter for two months, but it's never very cold.

8. _____ outside. Don't forget your umbrella.

Read this e-mail and complete the tasks below.

To: Lisa Miller
From: Jada Hal
Cc: Gina Flynn
Subject: Hello from school

Hi, guys!

I'm writing this on Chris's computer. He's studying in the library at the moment. Everything is fine. I'm taking three science classes this semester.

I don't have an apartment right now. For now I'm staying with Maria. Luisa and I are trying to get an apartment together. But the apartments seem very expensive. And rents are going up all the time.

Good-bye for now. My favorite TV show is starting. I'll call you this weekend.

Love,
Jada

Find sentences in the e-mail that are examples of the following uses. Write each sentence under the appropriate use.

1. The present continuous for an activity that is in progress at the exact moment the speaker is talking:

    a. _I'm writing this on Chris's computer._

    b. _____

    c. _____

2. The present continuous for an activity that is in progress but not happening at the exact moment the speaker is talking:

    a. _____

    b. _____

    c. _____

3. The present continuous for situations that are changing:

    _____

4. Stative verbs that are usually used in the simple present:

    a. _____

    b. _____

COMBINING FORM, MEANING, AND USE

Thinking About Meaning and Use

Complete these sentences. Write the simple present or the present continuous forms of the verbs in parentheses. Use contractions when possible.

1. Sasha _is driving_ (drive) the car, but he _doesn't own_ (not own) it.

2. They _____ (talk) to the teacher because they _____ (not/understand) the homework.

3. They _____ (build) a new library because the old library _____ (not/have) enough room.

4. Hector _____ (not/seem) very happy these days. Maybe he _____ (work) too hard.

5. He _____ (think) the chapter is easy, so he _____ (not study) for the grammar test.

6. _____ you _____ (know) Yoko? She _____ (act) in the new play.

Writing

Follow the steps below to write a descriptive paragraph. Write as much detail as you can. Use the present continuous when possible.

1. Look out a window that has a view of a street.

2. On a separate sheet of paper, write a paragraph describing what is happening. You may want to use some words from the box.

SUBJECTS	VERBS
some people a dog/cat/bird a group of students/children a truck/car	carrying holding moving (toward/away from . . .) reading laughing running standing (near/beside/at . . .)

It's raining, so there aren't many people outside. Two students are running toward the building. Maybe they're late for class . . . .

Chapters 1–3

A. Use each set of words to write the question for these question/answer jokes.

1. A: _____? (fish/go/heaven/to/what)

    B: Angel fish!

2. A: _____? (do/face/flowers/have/on/you/your/what)

    B: Tulips (two lips)!

3. A: _____? (old/an/die/does/clock/when)

    B: When its time is up!

4. A: _____? (words/have/the/letters/most/what)

    B: The words *post office*!

5. A: _____? (a/a/does/giraffe/have/long/neck/why)

    B: Because its feet smell bad!

6. A: _____? (a/does/doctor/get/angry/when)

    B: When he has no more patience (patients)!

B. Read these sentences about Saturday afternoon at Alex's house. Find and correct the errors.

7. Today is Saturday, and Alex is stay at home with his family.

8. His mother makes a chocolate cake in the kitchen.

9. The cake is smelling great.

10. His father is outside. He washes his car.

11. His sister, Tina, is listen to music in her bedroom.

12. She is playing it too loud, and Alex is hearing it in the basement.

13. His sister, Sara, is plays a video game in the living room.

14. Everybody is seeming very happy.

C. Complete these sentences with the correct word or phrase.

15. School _____ at 8:30 every day, so why are you late?
    a. starts   **b.** is starting   **c.** start

16. Excuse me. _____ anyone sitting here?
    a. Do   **b.** Is   **c.** Does

17. Flight 103 _____ at 5:00 every evening, according to the schedule.
    a. is leaving   **b.** does leave   **c.** leaves

18. Please _____ the flowers.
    a. not pick   **b.** not picking   **c.** don't pick

19. Right now, I _____ a bath.
    a. am taking   **b.** takes   **c.** take

20. Excuse me, how many cars _____ in the garage? Is there room for mine?
    a. fits   **b.** do fit   **c.** fit

21. Bring the umbrella! It _____ outside.
    a. rains   **b.** 's raining   **c.** rain

22. _____ your parents come from El Salvador?
    a. Are   **b.** Do   **c.** Does

23. The sign says "Danger: _____ enter."
    a. No   **b.** Do not   **c.** Not

24. My father _____ like tomatoes.
    a. doesn't   **b.** don't   **c.** isn't

25. Eva _____ the furniture once a week.
    a. is dusting   **b.** dust   **c.** dusts

26. Don't take that truck, Ben. It _____ to you.
    a. doesn't belong   **b.** don't belong   **c.** isn't belonging

27. I speak Spanish, but I _____ it.
    a. not write   **b.** not writing   **c.** don't write

28. The post office is on 9th Avenue. _____ right at the corner.
    a. Turn   **b.** Turning   **c.** Turns

29. _____ smoke here, please.
    a. Don't   **b.** No   **c.** Not

30. Oh, no! Look at the scale! I _____ 150 pounds!
    a. am weighing   **b.** weigh   **c.** weighs

4 The Simple Past

FORM

1 **Examining Form**

Read this magazine article and complete the tasks below.

Robin Williams

Robin Williams, actor

Robin Williams <u>was</u> an only child. His parents were wealthy; his father was an executive at the Ford Motor Company. His mother was often
5 busy. As a result, Robin spent a lot of time alone.

Robin was a good student. He (admired) his father and tried to please him by working hard in
10 school. Mr. Williams believed in discipline and hard work.

Robin went to college to study politics and economics. But during his first year he took an acting
15 class. He found that he loved the theater, and he was a good actor.

When Robin returned home after the spring semester, he nervously
20 told his father that he wanted to be an actor. His father wasn't very happy. He advised his son to learn a more useful skill.

1. There are seven examples of the past tense forms of *be* in the article. The first one is underlined. Underline six more.

2. There are seven examples of regular simple past verbs in the article. The first one is circled. Circle six more.

3. There are five examples of irregular simple past verbs in the article (not including *be*). The first one is boxed. Draw a box around four more.

Working on the Simple Past of *Be*

Complete this paragraph with *was* and *were*.

It <u>was</u> a beautiful day in late August. The clouds _____
$\quad$ 1 $\qquad\qquad\qquad\qquad\qquad\qquad\qquad\qquad\qquad$ 2

high in the sky. Best of all, the circus _____ in town. My brother and I
$\qquad\qquad\qquad\qquad\qquad\qquad$ 3

_____ very excited. This _____ something new for us. My
$\qquad$ 4 $\qquad\qquad\qquad\qquad\qquad$ 5

brother _____ interested in the elephants. They _____ old and
$\qquad\qquad\qquad$ 6 $\qquad\qquad\qquad\qquad\qquad\qquad\qquad$ 7

tired, but for him they _____ wonderful creatures.
$\qquad\qquad\qquad\qquad\qquad$ 8

Rewriting Statements in the Simple Past

Read what a student says about his favorite teacher and complete the task below.

```
    Mr. Kennedy is a great teacher. He teaches me English. I
learn  a  lot  in  his  class.  First,  he  explains  things
clearly. When two words have similar meanings, he shows us
the difference in a simple way. Time goes by quickly in his
class. We don't get bored.
    Mr. Kennedy doesn't have favorites. He spends time with
everyone.  He  doesn't  make  comments  about  the  weaker
students.  He  encourages  them  and  helps  them  a  lot.  He
knows everyone's name by the second class. He's everyone's
favorite teacher, and he really enjoys teaching.
```

What did the student say a year later? Rewrite the paragraphs, changing the simple present verbs to the simple past.

$\qquad$ *Mr. Kennedy was a great teacher. He taught me English . . . .*

_____

_____

_____

_____

_____

_____

4 Asking *Yes/No* Questions

Use the statements and the words in parentheses to write *Yes/No* questions.

1. I was born in Colombia.

   (your brother?) <u>Was your brother born in Colombia?</u>

2. I was very happy in Colombia.

   (your parents?) _____

3. I came to the U.S. in 1998.

   (your parents?) _____

4. My mother wanted to move to the U.S.

   (your father?) _____

5. I was very homesick at first.

   (your sisters?) _____

6. My mother found work.

   (your father?) _____

5 Asking Information Questions

Use the words in parentheses to write information questions for the answers below. Use the simple past.

1. Alexander Fleming discovered penicillin.

   a. (Alexander Fleming) <u>Who discovered penicillin?</u>

   b. (penicillin) <u>What did Alexander Fleming discover?</u>

2. Leonardo da Vinci painted the *Mona Lisa*.

   a. (the *Mona Lisa*) _____

   b. (Leonardo da Vinci) _____

3. The California Gold Rush began in 1848.

   a. (the California Gold Rush) _____

   b. (in 1848) _____

4. Nelson Mandela won the Nobel Peace Prize in 1993.

   a. (Nelson Mandela) _____

   b. (in 1993) _____

MEANING AND USE

6 Understanding Uses of the Simple Past

Read the sentences in the box about some events in one woman's life and complete the task below.

> **a.** As a child, Celia Clark was often sick for many months at a time.
>
> **b.** But every time her class had an exam, she got the best grade.
>
> **c.** She graduated from college on May 15, 1986.
>
> **d.** Last month she went to Peru.
>
> **e.** She got married last Sunday.

Match the events in Celia's life to the uses of the simple past. You may use a letter more than once.

1. an action or state in the distant past _a_ ____ ____

2. an action or state in the recent past ____ ____

3. an action or state that happened repeatedly ____ ____

4. an action or state that happened only once ____ ____ ____

7 Understanding *Used to*

Replace the underlined simple past verb forms with *used to* where appropriate and rewrite the sentences. In two sentences, *used to* is not appropriate. For these sentences, make no change.

1. My grandparents <u>had</u> a farm in Virginia.
   My grandparents used to have a farm in Virginia.

2. I <u>went</u> there every summer.
   _____

3. One summer my grandfather <u>asked</u> me to help him with work on the farm.
   _____

4. I <u>loved</u> working on the farm.
   _____

5. I <u>took</u> very good care of the animals.
   _____

6. One day my grandfather <u>taught</u> me to drive his tractor.
   _____

COMBINING FORM, MEANING, AND USE

8) Editing

There are twelve errors in this student's composition. The first one has been corrected. Find and correct eleven more.

>   *came*
> I ~~come~~ to the United States two years ago, when I was 15 years old. I was sad when I left my home country, especially when I say good-bye to my friends.
>
>   At the beginning, living in the U.S. isn't easy for me. In those days the language is hard for me because I don't speak it very well. Also, my parents don't speak English at all then, so I help them. A few months after I came here, I met some people who become my friends. This makes a big difference in my life at that time. After I meet them, I feel more confident.
>
>   Now I am going to school, I had some friends, and my English is better, too.

9) Writing

A. Think about your first day in a new place—for example, in a new country or a new school. Take notes on the following questions and on other details you remember:

- What was the new place?
- When was this?
- Who were you with?
- Why were you there?

- What happened?
- What did you think?
- How did you feel?
- Who did you meet?

B. On a separate sheet of paper, write a paragraph about your first day in the new place. Use your notes, and put events in the correct order. Use the simple past.

>   I remember the first day I went to my high school. I was still in eighth grade. My teacher took our class to the high school for a visit. . . .

The Past Continuous and Past Time Clauses

FORM

 Examining Form

Read this story and complete the task below.

Drama in the Air

It was impossible to sleep. The plane <u>was shaking</u> violently. The lights in the cabin were flashing, and the TV sets lost their pictures. 5 Something in the kitchen area fell to the floor with a loud crash. The flight attendant announced an emergency landing at Tokyo airport. Everybody was scared. A child was crying, and 10 some passengers were holding onto each other. I felt that the plane was going down, but I couldn't see anything because it was raining.

Fifteen minutes later, the plane 15 landed. I looked out the window. Ambulances and fire trucks were rushing toward us. When the plane finally came to a stop, the attendants opened all the emergency doors and 20 helped us get off the plane. Doctors were waiting to meet us. A few passengers had minor injuries, but I was OK. The next day, I took another plane to the United States.

There are eight examples of the past continuous in the story. The first one is underlined. Underline seven more.

Rewrite these sentences, changing the simple past verbs to the past continuous.

1. Fumiko wore a red dress.

   <u>Fumiko was wearing a red dress</u> when I met her.

2. We ate lunch in the cafeteria.

   _____ when we heard a crash in the kitchen.

3. You sat on the deck.

   _____ when I got here.

4. The sun shone.

   _____ when we left the house.

5. The boys walked to the park.

   _____ when it started to rain.

3 **Asking Information Questions**

Complete the conversation about a power blackout. Use the words and phrases to write information questions with the past continuous.

1. What / you / do / when the lights went out?

   Hector: <u>What were you doing when the lights went out?</u>

   Lisa: I was studying with a friend.

2. Who / you / study / with?

   Hector: _____

   Lisa: I was studying with Holly.

3. Where / you / study?

   Hector: _____

   Lisa: In the library.

4. Why / you / study?

   Hector: _____

   Lisa: Because we had an exam the next day.

5. Where / you / sit?

   Hector: _____

   Lisa: By the window.

Working on Past Time Clauses

Rewrite these sentences, changing the order of the clauses. Make changes as necessary.

1. When Amy looked out the window, she couldn't believe her eyes.

   Amy couldn't believe her eyes when she looked out the window.

2. We walked home after the rain stopped.

   _____

3. Keiko was exhausted when she got home.

   _____

4. After Hanna graduated from college, she moved to Los Angeles.

   _____

5. Paulo felt relaxed while he was on his vacation.

   _____

MEANING AND USE

5 **Understanding the Past Continuous and the Simple Past**

Choose the correct use of the past forms in each sentence.

1. We were watching TV when the lights went out.
   a. describes two simultaneous events
   (b.) describes one event interrupted by another

2. Last semester I was getting ready for an exam. My friend Holly and I were studying in the library. Suddenly...
   a. gives background information
   b. describes events in sequence

3. While I was eating, the phone rang.
   a. describes two simultaneous events
   b. describes one event interrupted by another

4. After Fred quit his job, he moved back to Ohio.
   a. describes one event interrupted by another
   b. describes events in sequence

5. Erica, I was thinking about you last night. I'm so glad you called.
   a. describes an activity in progress in the past
   b. gives background information

Choose the best answer to complete each sentence.

1. We went out to eat after _____.

    (a.) I finished my homework

    b. I was finishing my homework

2. While I was sleeping, _____.

    a. Paul was coming into the room

    b. Paul came into the room

3. I was living in Europe when _____.

    a. you grew up in New York City

    b. you were growing up in New York City

4. When we looked out the window, _____.

    a. it snowed

    b. it was snowing

5. _____ when I fell asleep.

    a. I was watching TV

    b. I watched TV

6. We opened the letter after _____.

    a. we received it

    b. we were receiving it

7. _____ when it cracked.

    a. Susan held the glass

    b. Susan was holding the glass

8. _____ when he fell.

    a. He was walking

    b. He walked

9. I was waiting at the airport when _____.

    a. I was hearing about the delay

    b. I heard about the delay

10. Ana left the party before _____.

    a. her sister came for her

    b. her sister was coming for her

Look at Bob's journal and complete the tasks below.

Wednesday, March 20	
8:55-9:30:	Read e-mail (9:20: the boss arrived)
9:30-10:00:	Prepared the conference room for a meeting
10:00-11:00:	Took notes in the meeting
11:00-11:15:	Made copies, then the copy machine broke
11:15-12:10:	Made phone calls (11:30: received a fax from New York office, but the fax machine jammed)
12:10-1:00:	Went to lunch (12:30: boss in a meeting)

A. Write T for *true* or F for *false* for each statement.

___F___ 1. The boss arrived at work before Bob did.

_____ 2. Bob was reading his e-mail when the boss arrived.

_____ 3. Before the meeting, Bob prepared the conference room.

_____ 4. Bob took notes before he prepared the conference room.

_____ 5. He made copies before he took notes in the meeting.

_____ 6. The copy machine broke after he made copies.

_____ 7. Before Bob made phone calls, the fax machine jammed.

_____ 8. The fax machine jammed after the copy machine broke.

_____ 9. While Bob was at lunch, his boss was in a meeting.

_____ 10. Bob went to lunch before he received a fax.

B. There are five false statements in part A. Rewrite the false statements as true statements. The first one has been done for you.

1. The boss arrived at work after Bob did.

_____

_____

_____

_____

_____

COMBINING FORM, MEANING, AND USE

Editing

There are six errors in this student's composition. The first one has been corrected. Find and correct five more.

>   *was walking*
>
> While I ~~walked~~ home from the Chinatown library yesterday, a strange thing happened to me. When I was reaching the corner of Broadway and Stockton, I stopped because the light was red. I was waiting for the light to change, and suddenly someone was tapping me once on my shoulder. Who was it? I turned around to find out. A man were standing behind me. When the light changed, I began to walk really fast. But every time I looked behind me, I was seeing the man. Finally, I went into a drugstore to escape from him. Ten minutes later I was coming out. The man was still outside! He came up to me and spoke. "Are you Susie Lin?" he asked. "I'm your cousin from Vancouver."

Writing

On a separate sheet of paper, answer the questions below to write a one-paragraph mystery story. Use the simple past, the past continuous, and past time clauses. Use your imagination!

1. First, give the background information: What time was it? Where were you? Who were you with? What were you doing, talking about, or thinking?

2. Then describe the action: What happened suddenly? What did you do? What did you see? What happened then?

3. Finally, tell how your story ends.

>   It was about nine o'clock on a Sunday evening. It was raining, and I was playing cards with my family. Suddenly, there was a loud noise outside the window. We ran to the window, and when we looked outside. . . .

CHAPTER

6 The Present Perfect

FORM

 1 Examining Form

Read this newspaper article and complete the tasks below.

Some Will Go the Extra Mile

Unlike most people, Marty O'Brien loves long car trips. In fact, he often tries to make them longer.

5 Marty is a member of the Extra Miler Club. His goal is to visit every one of the 3,145 counties in the United States. So far, he <u>has visited</u> 1,441. "On every trip," he says, "I 10 look for new places to go."

That's the philosophy of the people in the Extra Miler Club. The club began in 1973, and it now has 207 members. Twelve of these 15 members have visited every county. They have even traveled by

seaplane to get to counties in Alaska that are hard to reach. Some others have been to every state.

20 Roy Carson is one of the people who started the club. In 1985 he traveled to his last county. But he didn't take any photographs on his trips. So now he is trying again. 25 This time he is taking photographs of himself in front of each county sign. So far, he has covered 538,427 miles. "It's just as much fun the second time around, but it's a lot 30 more expensive," he says. Gas cost just 39 cents a gallon when he first started–in 1949.

---

county: a geographical and political division within a state in the U.S.

1. There are five examples of the present perfect in the article. The first one is underlined. Underline four more.

2. How is the present perfect formed? _____

Complete these questions with the past participles of the verbs in the box. Then answer the questions.

be	eat	find	fly	meet	ride

Have you ever . . .

1. __been__ on television? _No, I haven't._

2. _____ a horse? _____

3. _____ Indian food? _____

4. _____ a famous person? _____

5. _____ in a helicopter? _____

6. _____ money in the street? _____

3 **Asking Information Questions**

Use the words and phrases to write information questions in the present perfect.

1. How long / you / be / out of college?

     How long have you been out of college?

2. Where / you / travel / to?

     _____

3. How many people / she / invite?

     _____

4. Who / be / to China?

     _____

5. Why / you / choose / that book?

     _____

6. How long / Larry / live / there?

     _____

7. What / you / prepare / for lunch?

     _____

8. How much money / you / spend / this week?

     _____

MEANING AND USE

4 **Understanding the Present Perfect**

Choose the best answer to complete each sentence.

1. She's been a teacher all her life, _____.
   a. and she loved her job
   (b.) and she loves her job

2. I've traveled in Europe a lot, and in 2001 _____.
   a. I've gone to Africa
   b. I went to Africa

3. I've had that car for five years, _____.
   a. and it never breaks down
   b. and I sold it

4. We haven't eaten at the Greek restaurant yet, _____.
   a. so we tried it last night
   b. so we want to try it soon

5. We haven't solved the problem yet, _____.
   a. so we gave up
   b. but we aren't giving up

6. Pedro is one of my best friends; _____.
   a. I've known him for a long time
   b. I knew him for a long time

5 **Using *For* and *Since***

Complete these time expressions and time clauses with *for* or *since*.

1. _for_ three days

2. _____ 3 o'clock

3. _____ a long time

4. _____ a moment

5. _____ last month

6. _____ a month

7. _____ he was a boy

8. _____ 1988

Complete this conversation with the present perfect or simple past forms of the verbs in parentheses. Use contractions when possible.

A: Why do you want to work here?

B: Well, I _'ve loved_ (love) children all my life. I _____ (want) to work
$\quad$ 1 $\qquad\qquad$ 2

with kids since I _____ (leave) high school.
$\qquad$ 3

A: Your resume says that you _____ (work) in the childcare center at the
$\qquad$ 4

university from 1999 to 2001. Can you tell me about that?

B: Yes. It _____ (be) a part-time job. We _____ (play) with the
$\qquad$ 5 $\qquad\qquad$ 6

children and _____ (give) them lunch. I _____ (work) with a
$\qquad$ 7 $\qquad\qquad$ 8

Head Teacher.

A: Tell me about the jobs you _____ (have) since then. _____ (you/
$\qquad$ 9 $\qquad\qquad$ 10

ever have) full responsibility for children in your care?

B: Yes. For the last year I _____ (look after) one-year-old twins.
$\qquad$ 11

Use the words below to rewrite each sentence in two ways. Do not change the meaning of the sentence. More than one answer may be possible.

1. I haven't seen a volcano in my whole life.

already	never	still	so far	yet

$\quad$ **a.** _I've never seen a volcano._

$\quad$ **b.** _I haven't seen a volcano yet._

2. Up to now, we've raised $5,700.

$\quad$ **a.** _____

$\quad$ **b.** _____

3. He hasn't been to Europe.

$\quad$ **a.** _____

$\quad$ **b.** _____

4. They've interviewed five people.

$\quad$ **a.** _____

$\quad$ **b.** _____

COMBINING FORM, MEANING, AND USE

There are nine errors in these paragraphs. The first one has been corrected. Find and correct eight more.

> _traveled_
> My wife and I have ~~travel~~ as much as possible since we retired. We've visited cousins in Australia, and we been to New Zealand twice. We've also went on safari in Africa. We've been to Europe a lot. Gina and I has spent time in Paris, in Madrid, and in several cities in Italy. We haven't to Eastern Europe yet, though. We hope to visit Prague and Budapest next year.
>
> My sister Betty was born in the United States, and she has never traveled outside the country–except once when she was very young. But she have been to a lot of places in the U.S. She has visit most of the national parks: the Grand Canyon, Yellowstone, Yosemite, and so on. She has been to all of the big cities, too. In fact, she is lived in four different cities in the U.S.: New York, Boston, Los Angeles, and San Francisco. I think she seen more of her own country than most people.

On a separate sheet of paper, write a paragraph about your travel experiences. Use the present perfect or the simple past as needed.

1. In your first few sentences, describe your travel experience in general.

2. In the rest of the paragraph, describe one or more trips in particular. Use the questions below to help you write your paragraph:
   - How many countries or cities have you visited?
   - Have you visited any places more than once?
   - Where did you go on a recent trip?
   - Think of places you haven't visited. Which ones would you like to visit?

> I haven't traveled very much outside my country, but I have visited different areas in my country. For example, I've been to Chiang Mai in northern Thailand several times. My last visit to Chiang Mai was last year. . . .

Chapters 4–6

A. Complete the sentences with the correct form of the verbs in the box.

begin	bite	buy	eat	fall	fly	give	grow	hear	lose	say	sell	throw	wear

1. Who _____ , "I have a dream" in 1963?

2. Myles _____ the ball, and Carl caught it.

3. Julie Morgan? Who was she? I've never _____ of her.

4. Amelia Earhart _____ a small plane across the Atlantic in 1932.

5. We went to the store and _____ everything for the party.

6. You're late! The movie has already _____ .

7. Our neighbors _____ their house and moved to Idaho.

8. Have you ever _____ frogs' legs?

9. I've never _____ this jacket before. Does it look OK?

10. She wasn't finished with the test, so we _____ her more time.

11. She hurt her knee when she _____ off her bike.

12. You're such a big girl! You've _____ a lot since the last time I saw you.

13. Ow! That dog _____ me!

14. Have you seen my keys? I've _____ them again.

B. Read these sentences. Check (✓) *OK* if the sentence is logical or *NOT OK* if the sentence is not logical.

	OK	NOT OK
15. Paul was a carpenter for ten years, and he loves it.		
16. We lived in Atlanta for five years.		
17. She's worked here for six years before she left in July.		
18. After I heard the news, I went straight to the hospital.		
19. While he was taking a shower, he got dressed.		
20. After I fell asleep, I read the newspaper.		
21. I haven't seen Lee since yesterday.		

C. Choose the correct word or phrase to complete each sentence.

22. How long ____ you been here?

    a. are   **b.** did   **c.** have

23. ____ you home last night?

    a. Are   **b.** Did   **c.** Were

24. After our guests ____, we sat down to dinner.

    a. arrived   **b.** were arriving   **c.** have arrived

25. Who ____ to when I saw you yesterday?

    a. you talk   **b.** are you talking   **c.** were you talking

26. Where have you been? I haven't seen you ____ a long time!

    a. at   **b.** for   **c.** since

27. We've ____ finished phase one of the project.

    a. already   **b.** still   **c.** yet

28. We ____ go there often when we were children, but we do now.

    a. used to   **b.** didn't use   **c.** didn't use to

29. My father ____ Silvio since they were kids.

    a. knows   **b.** has known   **c.** knew

30. We were all very upset ____ we heard the bad news.

    a. during   **b.** when   **c.** while

Future Time: *Be Going To*, *Will*, and the Present Continuous

FORM

1 **Examining Form**

Read this letter and complete the tasks below.

To: Lisa Miller
From: Jada Hal
Cc: Gina Flynn
Subject: New address

---

5 Hi everyone!

Great news! Luisa and I have found an apartment! We're moving in next Saturday. My new address <u>will be</u>:

235 New St. #6
Berkeley, CA 94703

10 It's a really nice apartment. It's small, but it's really close to campus, so we can walk to school. It's a little more expensive than we expected, but we won't need to take the bus, so we'll save some money there. We'll also save money by eating at home more. I'm looking forward to having our own place. I'm sure Luisa will be a great roommate. She's (going to cook,) and I'm going to clean. It's all arranged!

15 We don't have a lot of furniture, but Luisa's brother is going to give us some of his old furniture, so we'll be all set. He's going to help us move, too!

Anyway, I have to go now. I'll write again soon.

Love,
Jada

---

1. There are four examples of the future with *be going to* in the letter. The first one is circled. Circle three more.

2. There are seven examples of the future with *will* in the letter. The first one is underlined. Underline six more. One of the examples is negative.

3. There is one example of the present continuous as future. Draw a box around it.

Working on Statements and Questions with *Be Going To*

Use the words and phrases to write conversations with *be going to.* Use contractions when possible.

Conversation 1

1. **Jenny:** we / get married in the spring.

   <u>We're going to get married in the spring.</u>

2. **Ana:** you / have a big wedding?

   _____

3. **Jenny:** No. We / not / have a big celebration.

   _____

Conversation 2

4. **Myles:** it / rain tomorrow?

   _____

5. **Eric:** Yes. What / you / do?

   _____

6. **Myles:** I / stay home and read a book.

   _____

Asking Information Questions with *Will*

Write information questions about the underlined phrases. Use *will.*

1. <u>Where will you meet me?</u>

   I'll meet you <u>at the tennis courts</u>.

2. _____

   He'll find out the results <u>on Tuesday</u>.

3. _____

   We'll go <u>to the movies</u>.

4. _____

   <u>Ms. Santiago</u> will be there.

5. _____

   The photos will be ready <u>at noon</u>.

6. _____

   It will take <u>almost four hours</u>.

4 Rewriting Affirmative and Negative Statements with *Will*

Read what Gary's friend says about Gary's daily routine and complete the task below.

> My friend Gary has never heard of the expression "Variety is the spice of life." Every day Gary gets up at 6:00, puts on shorts and a T-shirt, and goes out for a run. He gets back at 6:45, takes a shower, and shaves. He goes downstairs at 7:00. He makes a cup of coffee, but he doesn't drink it. He takes it with him in his car. He doesn't eat anything, either. Then he drives to work. He has breakfast at his desk.

If Gary does the same things every day, what will he do tomorrow? Rewrite the paragraph, using *will*. Use contractions when possible.

　　　　My friend Gary will get up at 6:00, put on shorts and a T-shirt, and go out for a run.

_____

_____

_____

_____

_____

MEANING AND USE

5 Understanding *Will*

A. Match each statement to a place or situation.

 _d_ **1.** I won't tell Mom.　　　　　　　**a.** on the phone

 ____ **2.** This will hurt a little.　　　　　**b.** on TV or the radio

 ____ **3.** I'll have the steak.　　　　　　**c.** in a store

 ____ **4.** I'll buy that one.　　　　　　　**d.** at home

 ____ **5.** I'll give her the message.　　　　**e.** at the doctor's office

 ____ **6.** Rain showers will begin this evening.　**f.** in a restaurant

B. How is each statement in part A used? Write the number of the statement next to the appropriate use below.

 a. a promise: _1_ ____

 b. a prediction: ____ ____

 c. a decision: ____ ____

6 Understanding *Be Going To* and the Present Continuous

Read this conversation and complete the tasks below.

Larry: Are you and Kate having a good vacation here in Colorado?

Paul: We're having a wonderful time. It's so nice here. We don't want to go home.

Larry: When are you leaving?

Paul: Next week. We're leaving here on Wednesday. Then we're flying home on Sunday.

Larry: Where are you going in between?

Paul: We're going to visit some friends in Boulder for a few days.

Larry: Well, come for dinner before you leave. What are you doing tomorrow?

Paul: I think we're going to hike up the mountain.

Larry: Really? Are you sure? They say the weather's going to be bad. You're going to get very wet. Why don't you spend the day with Julie and me in Aspen instead?

Write the questions and statements from the conversation that show the following uses:

1. *be going to* to talk about future plans or intentions

   a. <u>We're going to visit some friends in Boulder for a few days.</u>

   b. _____

2. *be going to* to make predictions

   a. _____

   b. _____

3. the present continuous to talk about future plans or intentions

   a. _____

   b. _____

   c. _____

   d. _____

   e. _____

4. the present continuous to talk about the present

   a. _____

   b. _____

Look at these pairs of sentences. Write *S* if they have the same meaning. Write *D* if their meanings are different.

1. __D__ What are you doing?

   What are you going to do?

2. _____ We're getting married next month.

   We're going to get married next month.

3. _____ She's losing weight.

   She's going to lose weight.

4. _____ We're not going on vacation this year.

   We're not going to go on vacation this year.

5. _____ Are you working this evening?

   Are you going to work this evening?

6. _____ My boss is getting mad at me.

   My boss is going to get mad at me.

COMBINING FORM, MEANING, AND USE

8 **Thinking About Meaning and Use**

Choose the correct sentence to complete each conversation.

1. **A:** What are your plans for summer vacation?

   B: _____

   a. I'll spend a month in Hawaii.

   b. I'm going to spend a month in Hawaii.

2. **A:** What are you guys doing this afternoon?

   B: _____

   a. We'll play tennis.

   b. We're going to play tennis.

3. **A:** Oh, no! That's the phone.

   B: _____

   a. I'll get it.

   b. I'm going to get it.

4. **A:** I want to sell my sofa.

   B: _____

   a. I'll give you $30 for it.

   b. I'm giving you $30 for it.

5. **A:** Why are you buying a German dictionary?

   B: _____

   a. I'll study German.

   b. I'm going to study German.

6. **A:** What time do you leave?

   B: _____

   a. I'll take the 5:00 bus.

   b. I'm taking the 5:00 bus.

A. Imagine you are taking a trip to Egypt next week. Read the itinerary below.

B. On a separate sheet of paper, write a one-paragraph e-mail to a friend about the trip. Using information from the itinerary, tell about your plans and make some predictions. Express future time with the present continuous and *will* as appropriate.

Globe Travel • **202 Sanford Avenue** • **Newark, NJ 07039**

Travel Itinerary

Day 1 – Saturday	Leave the U.S. for Europe.
Day 2 – Sunday	Arrive in Frankfurt. Leave that evening for Cairo. On arrival, we take you to your hotel.
Day 3 – Monday	Cairo. Get up early for a visit to the Pyramids and the Egyptian Museum. In the afternoon, take a drive through Old Cairo.
Day 4 – Tuesday	Cairo/Nile Cruise. Fly to the Aswan Dam and board your cruise ship.
Days 5-8 – Wednesday-Saturday	Nile Cruise. See beautiful views of the River Nile. Visit old temples during the day and relax on the boat at night.
Day 9 – Sunday	Return to Cairo.
Day 10 – Monday	Fly back to the U.S.

To: Kevin Ross
From: Paul Lee
Cc:
Subject: Trip to Egypt

Hi Kevin,

I'm going on a ten-day trip to Egypt! We're leaving on Saturday and flying into Frankfurt.

Sunday morning. . . .

8 Future Time Clauses and *If* Clauses

FORM

Read the article and complete the tasks below.

A Polish Tradition

All parents wonder about their children's future. Will the infant sleeping peacefully in her crib become a doctor, a teacher, or a 5 future president? Many Polish families follow an old tradition to determine what kind of person their child will turn into. On the child's first birthday, the parents set several 10 objects on a table. For example, they may set out a book, a piece of bread, a set of car keys, and a musical instrument. They then sit the child at the table. Which object will 15 the child touch first?

If the child touches the book, she will be a good student. If the child reaches for the car keys, he will travel far. If the child goes for the 20 bread, she will love food. And if he touches the musical instrument, he will become a musician, of course!

1. Underline the main clauses in the second paragraph. What tense is used?

   _____

2. What tense is used in the dependent (future/*if*) clauses? _____

Completing Sentences with Future Time Clauses and *If* Clauses

Use the words or phrases to complete each sentence with a future time clause or a main clause. Use contractions when possible.

1. (if / I / finish / work early) <u>If I finish work early</u>, I'll go to a movie.

2. (we / eat / dinner) _____ when your father gets home.

3. Before I pay any more bills, _____ (I / cash / my paycheck).

4. Mr. Owens is going to retire _____ (when / he / turn / 68).

5. (I / not be / upset) _____ if you tell me the truth.

6. After the game is over, _____ (we / celebrate).

7. (I / buy / a new car) _____ if I get a raise.

8. (if / you / drive / too fast) _____, you'll have an accident.

3 **Rewriting Sentences with Future Time Clauses and *If* Clauses**

Rewrite these sentences, changing the order of the clauses. Use correct punctuation.

1. We're going to go shopping tonight if the stores stay open.

   <u>If the stores stay open, we're going to go shopping tonight.</u>

2. After I say good-bye to the children, I'll be ready to leave.

   _____

3. Sun-hee will be angry if we don't invite Eric to the party.

   _____

4. We're going to pick up the car when Victor gets here.

   _____

5. If the water's too cold, I'm not going to go swimming.

   _____

6. Dinner will be ready when the guests arrive.

   _____

7. They'll buy a bigger house if they have another baby.

   _____

8. After I graduate, I'll look for a job in San Francisco.

   _____

MEANING AND USE

Complete these sentences with future time clauses, *if* clauses, or main clauses.

1. <u>I will be very happy</u> when I finish this course.

2. I will study for the test before _____.

3. I will see my family when _____.

4. I will get a job after _____.

5. _____ if you help me study.

6. I will go on vacation if _____.

7. Before the day is over _____.

8. After I finish this exercise _____.

5 **Understanding *If* Clauses**

Read the sentences in the box. How is each one used? Write the letter of each sentence next to the appropriate use below.

> **a.** I'll call you if I get an answer.
>
> **b.** If you don't hurry up, you're going to miss the train.
>
> **c.** You won't get sick if you drink lots of water.
>
> **d.** If you wait here, I'll introduce you to Nesha.
>
> **e.** If Kane wins the election, he'll be a good mayor.
>
> **f.** They won't let you in if you don't have your card.
>
> **g.** If you ask the driver, he'll tell you when to get off.
>
> **h.** If it gets colder, it will probably snow.

1. a prediction: _e_ _____

2. a promise: _____ _____

3. a warning: _____ _____

4. advice: _____ _____

Choose the correct sentence to complete each conversation.

1. **Betty:** This coat might not go on sale.

    Kedra: _____

          (a.) Well, if it goes on sale, I'll buy it.

          b. Well, when it goes on sale, I'll buy it.

2. **Hiro:** We're definitely coming this evening.

    Eva: _____

          a. If you come, I'll introduce you to my parents.

          b. When you come, I'll introduce you to my parents.

3. **Mark:** If we take a trip to the beach next week, do you want to come?

    Tomek: _____

          a. When will you decide about the trip?

          b. When did you decide about the trip?

4. **Rick:** _____

    Gina: Thanks! I'll be ready.

          a. If I go to work tomorrow, I'll give you a ride.

          b. When I go to work tomorrow, I'll give you a ride.

COMBINING FORM, MEANING, AND USE

Combine each pair of sentences, using the words in parentheses. Make any necessary changes. Use correct punctuation. More than one answer is possible.

1. I'll see you tomorrow. Then I'll give you the book. (when)

    When I see you tomorrow, I'll give you the book.

    OR I'll give you the book when I see you tomorrow.

2. Reiko will do well in the interview. Then she'll get the job. (if)

    _____

3. I'm going to join a gym. Then I'm going to lose ten pounds. (after)

    _____

4. The movie will end. Then I'll call you. (when)

    _____

5. We'll make too much noise. Then the baby will wake up. (if)

_____

6. We're going to eat dinner. Then we'll listen to the radio. (before)

_____

7. Matt will buy the groceries. Then he will go to the bank. (after)

_____

8. Ana will read more books. Then she will increase her vocabulary. (if)

_____

8 **Writing**

Read about Elena's situation and complete the task below.

> Elena is 25 years old. She lives at home with her parents. She has lived in the same town all her life, and she has a lot of friends there. She works 40 hours a week in an office. The job pays a good salary, but it's boring. She probably won't be able to get a better job in her small town.
>
> A large company in a city has offered Elena a job. It's a much better job: It's more interesting, and it pays more. But it will also be more stressful. Elena will have to leave home and find an apartment in a city where she doesn't know anyone. Elena isn't sure if she should take the job.

Imagine you are Elena. On a separate sheet of paper, write a two- or three-paragraph letter to a friend to describe different possibilities and predictions about your situation. What will happen if you stay at your old job? What will happen if you take the new job? Use _if_ clauses or future time clauses when possible.

Dear Yuji,

    I was offered a job in the city, but I'm not sure what to do. If I stay at my old job, I will be close to my family... .

Chapters 7–8

A. Find and correct the error in each of these sentences.

1. I'll meeting John after work.

2. We not going to Los Angeles this summer.

3. I have an idea: I'm pick you up on my way to the airport.

4. Can you turn off the light after you are leaving the room?

5. Will you being at the party tomorrow?

6. When she will arrive home, she will phone her mother.

7. I going to tell you something.

8. This test isn't being easy.

B. Complete each response.

9. **Eva:** When are you going out?

   Paul: After _____ .

   a. I'll finish my homework

   b. I finish my homework

10. **Sasha:** Why are you still here'?

    Hector: I need to finish my work before _____ .

    a. I'm going home

    b. I go home

11. **Kim:** I'm going to bake a cake for the party.

    Sam: _____ , I'll make some cookies.

    a. If you bake a cake

    b. If you baked a cake

12. **Sandra:** I'm not feeling well.

    Ann: You'll feel better _____ .

    a. if you lie down

    b. if you're going to lie down

13. **Lee:** I think we're going to be late.

    Kedra: Well, if we leave now, _____ .

    a. we'll be on time

    b. we are on time

14. **Rita:** It's going to rain. You'll get wet!

    Nesha: If it rains, _____ .

    a. I used my umbrella

    b. I'll use my umbrella

15. **Maria:** Is Megan coming with us?

    Bill: Yes, _____ .

    a. if we drive there

    b. if we drove there.

16. **Keiko:** I'm going to the meeting now.

    Ana: Wait, _____ with you.

    a. I come

    b. I'll come

C. Choose the correct word or phrase to complete each sentence.

17. What _____ to do when you graduate?
    a. are you going   **b.** are going   **c.** you are going

18. If you take vitamins every day, you _____ get sick.
    a. aren't   **b.** not going to   **c.** won't

19. Have you heard the news? Tony and Diane _____ married!
    a. get   **b.** getting   **c.** are getting

20. The phone's ringing. I _____ it if you want.
    a. answer   **b.** 'll answer   **c.** 'm going to answer

21. I'll give Ms. Baxter the message when she _____ back.
    a. comes   **b.** will come   **c.** is going to come

22. If you don't drive more slowly, you _____ an accident.
    a. have   **b.** are having   **c.** are going to have

23. What _____ when they find out?
    a. your parents say   **b.** will your parents say   **c.** are your parents saying

24. I know it's a secret. Don't worry, I _____ a word.
    a. don't say   **b.** won't say   **c.** 'm not saying

25. I won't be home for dinner. I _____ with some people from school.
    a. 'm going out   **b.** go out   **c.** 'll go out

26. If you guys _____ that window, your father will be furious.
    a. break   **b.** will break   **c.** are breaking

27. If it breaks, I _____ you.
    a. call   **b.** 'll call   **c.** called

28. If you put on a hat, you _____ cold.
    a. aren't getting   **b.** not getting   **c.** won't get

29. I can't wait! I _____ on vacation next week.
    a. 'll be   **b.** being   **c.** be

30. Where _____ in Paris?
    a. you'll be   **b.** you are   **c.** will you be

Modals of Ability and Possibility

FORM

 Examining Form

Miguel is planning a surprise birthday party for his friend Rosa, and Kalin is helping him. Read this e-mail that Miguel sent Kalin, and complete the tasks below.

To: Kalin Jones
From: Miguel Ortiz
Cc:
Subject: Rosa's birthday party

Hi Kalin,

I reserved a private room at Charlie's Restaurant for Rosa's surprise birthday party on Thursday. The restaurant has two dining rooms, but I <u>couldn't</u> get the larger room because it was already reserved. The manager said that the other room can hold around 25 people, so it will be large

5 enough.

I've already talked with some of Rosa's friends. Most said they will come. Carlos and Alex may come, but they aren't sure. Kim is out of town, and she probably won't be back in time for the party.

Can you help me with a few more things before Thursday? I might not have time to do them. For example, can you order the birthday cake? There could be a lot of people, so order a large cake.

10 Thanks a lot,

Miguel

---

1. There are ten examples of modals in the e-mail. The first one is underlined. Underline nine more.

2. Check the correct statement. Correct the incorrect statement.

   _____ Each modal has only one form.

   _____ Modals agree with the subject.

2   Working on Modals of Present and Past Ability

A. Rewrite these sentences, using *can*. Make all the necessary changes.

1. My father speaks Russian.

   <u>My father can speak Russian.</u>

2. I don't ski.

   _____

3. Do you drive?

   _____

4. They play several instruments.

   _____

B. Rewrite these sentences, using *could*. Make all the necessary changes.

1. We didn't see anything.

   _____

2. Did you play the piano when you were younger?

   _____

3. They didn't tell me anything.

   _____

4. Did Tomek understand that?

   _____

3   Working on Modals of Future Possibility

A. Use the words and phrases to write information questions with *could*.

1. **Emily:** Let's go somewhere tomorrow.

   Steve: OK. Where / go?

   <u>Where could we go?</u>

2. **Miguel:** Let's ask Young-soo to pick us up in his car.

   Sara: When / get here?

   _____

3. **Pedro:** It will take some time.

   Teresa: How long / take?

   _____

4. Gary: I hope nothing goes wrong.

   Hanna: What / go wrong?

   _____

B. Use the words and phrases to write information questions with *will*.

1. Victor: I'm going to buy a new car.

   Megan: What kind / get?

   _____

2. Rita: I don't have much money this month.

   Susan: How / pay / your rent?

   _____

3. Tony: Steve's leaving for Las Vegas this morning.

   Kevin: What time / get / there?

   _____

4. Julie: I'm meeting some friends at the restaurant.

   Gary: Who / be / there?

   _____

MEANING AND USE

4 **Using Modals of Future Ability**

Complete these sentences with *can/can't* or *will be able to/won't be able to*.

1. If I work on this for the next two months, maybe I _'ll be able to_ understand it.

2. People _____ travel great distances in outer space now, but maybe in the future they _____ .

3. We _____ go to a restaurant this evening if you want to eat out.

4. The post office down the street is closing next month, so we _____ go there much longer.

5. After the operation, you _____ see very well for a few days. But you _____ see much better in a few weeks.

6. When the new bridge opens, we _____ drive to the city in less than an hour.

Understanding Modals of Past Ability

Do these sentences about the past use *could* correctly? Check (✓) *Correct* or *Incorrect*.
Then correct the incorrect sentences with *be able to.*

	CORRECT	INCORRECT
1. After he talked to her, he ~~could~~ *was able to* find out what was wrong.		✓
2. I could feel the excitement in the room as soon as I walked in.		
3. She failed the exam the first time, but after she studied she could pass.		
4. We couldn't see a thing when we arrived at the top.		
5. They could visit Lee in the hospital yesterday.		

Understanding Modals of Future Possibility

Read these sentences about Keiko's evening. Then write each boldfaced action in the
correct column of the chart.

1. Keiko will **go out tonight.**

2. She'll **eat dinner.**

3. Maybe she will **study English.**

4. She may **read a book.**

5. She could **watch TV.**

6. She'll **go to bed before midnight.**

	LESS CERTAINTY	MORE CERTAINTY
1.		go out tonight
2.		
3.		
4.		
5.		
6.		

COMBINING FORM, MEANING, AND USE

Complete these sentences with the correct modals.

1. When I was younger, I _____ understand a lot of Italian.

   a. can   **b.** could   **c.** might

2. We _____ get the tickets yesterday because Kevin waited in line for three hours.

   a. can   **b.** were able to   **c.** will be able to

3. I'm not sure where Dan will be tomorrow. He _____ be in London.

   a. can   **b.** may   **c.** will

4. He doesn't know much English now, but after he lives in the United States for a few months, he _____ understand much more.

   a. can   **b.** was able to   **c.** will be able to

5. Now you _____ buy stamps from ATM machines.

   a. can   **b.** might   **c.** may

6. It was dark when we arrived, so we _____ see anything.

   a. can't   **b.** couldn't   **c.** may not

A. Think about how transportation will be different in the future. Think about the following topics:

- crowded roads
- bicycles and motorcycles
- electric cars and buses
- high-speed trains
- space travel

B. On a separate sheet of paper, write a paragraph that describes how transportation might be different 50 years from now. Use some of these modals: *will/may/might/could/be able to.*

> Transportation could be very different 50 years from now. There will be a lot more people, especially in the cities. For that reason, public transportation might be... .

10 Modals and Phrases of Request, Permission, Desire, and Preference

FORM

1 Examining Form

Read these sentences from three telephone conversations and complete the tasks below.

__C__ 1. "Express Air. <u>May</u> I help you?"

_____ 2. "Could you hold on a minute? I'll check the fares."

_____ 3. "He's not home yet. Can I take a message?"

_____ 4. "What would you like to drink?"

_____ 5. "Would you prefer to fly on a weekend?"

_____ 6. "I'd like to change my order."

_____ 7. "Can I speak to Paolo, please?"

_____ 8. "I'd prefer the crispy noodles with that."

_____ 9. "Could you tell him I called?"

_____10. "I'd rather fly into London if that's possible."

---

1. Match the sentences above to *Conversations A, B,* or *C*:

   • *Conversation A:* Someone is ordering food from a restaurant.

   • *Conversation B:* Someone is taking a message.

   • *Conversation C:* Someone is talking with an airline representative about a flight reservation.

2. Underline the modal or phrase of request, permission, desire, or preference in each sentence.

2) Making Requests and Asking for Permission

Use the words to write questions. Use correct punctuation.

1. you / take / could / suitcases / those

   Could you take those suitcases?

2. I / coffee / more / some / have / may

   _____

3. you / take / would / picture / my

   _____

4. when / see / could / I / tomorrow / you

   _____

5. have / I / can / eat / something / to

   _____

6. me / you / will / give / a / ride

   _____

3) Working on *Would Like, Would Prefer,* and *Would Rather*

Rewrite these sentences using the words in parentheses. Make other changes and add *not* as necessary. Keep the meaning the same. Use contractions when possible.

1. Do you want to stay home tonight? (would rather)

   Would you rather stay home tonight?

2. I don't want to take a class on Fridays. (would prefer)

   _____

3. What time does Takeshi want to leave? (would like)

   _____

4. My mother doesn't want to come with us. (would rather)

   _____

5. Do you want milk or juice? (would prefer)

   _____

6. I want to live in a big city. (would like)

   _____

MEANING AND USE

Understanding Modals of Request and Permission

Rewrite each request in two ways for the situations given. Use the modals *can, would,* and *may*. More than one answer may be possible for each.

1. I'd like to speak with Carol.

   a. You're calling Carol at home: <u>Can I speak with Carol?</u>

   b. You're calling Carol at work: <u>May I speak with Carol, please?</u>

2. I'd like to talk to you after class.

   a. You say this to your classmate: _____

   b. You say this to your teacher: _____

3. Say that again.

   a. You say this to your brother: _____

   b. You say this to a stranger: _____

4. Drop me off at the corner.

   a. You say this to the bus driver: _____

   b. You say this to your friend: _____

Understanding Desires, Requests, Offers, and Preferences

Complete the conversations with *would like, would prefer,* and *would rather*. Use contractions when possible. More than one answer may be possible.

At home

Stefan: <u>Would</u> you <u>rather</u> stay home or go out to dinner tonight?

Irina: I think I _____ to go out rather than stay at home. How about you?

Stefan: I _____ go out, too. We could go to our favorite Chinese restaurant or try that new Italian restaurant.

Irina: I think tonight I _____ to try the Italian restaurant.

At the restaurant

Waiter: _____ you _____ some dessert now?

Irina: Yes, I _____ the cheesecake, please.

Waiter: And you, sir. _____ you _____ to have the cheesecake or the ice cream?

Stefan: I'm not having dessert. Thank you. But I _____ the check, please.

COMBINING FORM, MEANING, AND USE

Choose the correct word or phrase to complete each sentence.

1. May I _____ you?

   a. help   **b.** to help   **c.** helping

2. I don't have any money. _____ lend me five dollars?

   a. May you   **b.** Would you   **c.** Would you rather

3. **A:** May we use dictionaries?

   B: Yes, you _____ .

   a. may   **b.** could   **c.** would

4. **A:** Could you drive me home this evening?

   B: I'd like to, but I _____ .

   a. can't   **b.** couldn't   **c.** won't

5. **A:** _____ a cup of coffee?

   B: Yes, please.

   a. Would you rather   **b.** Do you like   **c.** Would you like

6. **A:** Would you let me know when it's ready?

   B: Yes, I _____ .

   a. would   **b.** will   **c.** can

7. I'd prefer _____ .

   a. stay home   **b.** to stay home   **c.** stayed home

8. **A:** Would you like to leave early or stay late?

   B: I'd _____ leave early.

   a. like   **b.** prefer   **c.** rather

9. **A:** Who got the job?

   B: I _____ say.

   a. wouldn't rather   **b.** would rather not   **c.** had rather not

10. Would you rather _____ now?

   a. not leave   **b.** not to leave   **c.** don't leave

Imagine that you need to change your work schedule because you want to take a computer course. On a separate sheet of paper, write two notes, one to your boss, Kedra, and one to your co-worker, Won-joon.

1. In your note to Kedra, request the schedule change and say when you want to work and why.

2. In your note to Won-joon, ask him to work for you next Tuesday. That's the day you have to register for the class. Ask him to call you at home if he can't do it.

Include some of these modals and modal phrases: *can, could, would, may, would prefer, would rather* and *would like.* Make sure that your note to Kedra is more formal than your note to Won-joon.

Dear Kedra,

    I would like to change my schedule in a couple of weeks because... .

Hi Won-joon,

    Can you work for me next Tuesday? ... .

CHAPTER 11

Modals and Phrasal Modals of Advice, Necessity, and Prohibition

FORM

 Examining Form

Read this magazine article and complete the tasks below.

Weird and Wonderful Hobbies

Many people these days are collecting everything and anything. And they're having fun doing it.

What ⓢhould you <u>collect</u>? The answer depends on your interests. You could collect old magazines, postcards, toys, buttons, posters, dolls... . The list is endless. But if you're going to start collecting something, there are a few points you must consider. First, you should try to focus on one specific area of interest. For example, bottle collecting is a popular hobby. But you'd better choose one special kind of bottle to collect, or your house will be full of glass in no time.

Next, you should learn everything you can about your hobby. This way you won't waste time or money collecting worthless items. For example, if you collect old postcards, you ought to know that of the millions of postcards from before 1914, only about five percent are worth anything. If you want to be a successful collector, you have to know how to recognize the valuable ones.

Finally, don't let money be your main reason for collecting. Collecting should be fun and educational, just like any other hobby.

1. There are nine examples of modals and phrasal modals of advice and necessity in the article. The first one is circled. Circle eight more.

2. Underline the verb that goes with each modal.

Working on Modals and Phrasal Modals

Complete these sentences with *go* or *to go.*

1. I think we should _go_____ to Janet's party.

2. We have _____ to work before 7:00.

3. You've got _____ to bed right now.

4. You'd better not _____ there too early.

5. Amy should _____ to school today.

6. We really must _____ right now.

7. Josh has _____ to the doctor in the morning.

8. The children ought _____ swimming tomorrow.

9. You'd better _____ now.

10. Celia's got _____ home for dinner.

Writing Information Questions with Modals and Phrasal Modals

Write information questions about the underlined words.

1. We have to buy <u>a present</u>.
   _What do we have to buy?_____

2. She should tell <u>a teacher</u>.
   _____

3. They have to leave <u>next week</u>.
   _____

4. I have to stay <u>for an hour</u>.
   _____

5. He has to tell her <u>soon</u>.
   _____

6. Emily should do <u>something</u>.
   _____

7. You should ask <u>Celia</u>.
   _____

8. We should exercise <u>every day</u>.
   _____

Choosing Modals and Phrasal Modals of Advice and Necessity

Choose the correct word or phrase to complete each sentence.

1. You _____ let the baby put that in his mouth.

   a. couldn't   **b.** shouldn't

2. What kind of gift _____ get for my girlfriend?

   a. ought I   **b.** should I

3. We _____ get up early tomorrow.

   a. doesn't have to   **b.** don't have to

4. When do you _____ be at the airport?

   a. have to   **b.** must

5. You _____ to eat more vegetables.

   a. had better   **b.** ought

6. _____ to call my parents.

   a. I must   **b.** I've got

MEANING AND USE

5 **Understanding Modals and Phrasal Modals of Advice and Necessity**

Read this conversation. There are five examples of errors with modals and phrasal modals. The first one has been corrected. Find and correct four more. Some errors can be corrected in more than one way.

Satomi: I'm a little nervous about coming to the United States for the first time. What happens at the airport?

Chris: Well, everybody who is coming in from overseas had better go through [*has to/has got to*] Customs and Immigration. You could show your passport and your visa.

Satomi: OK. And how do I get from the airport to the university?

Chris: Well, you have to take public transportation, but it's probably better to take a taxi.

Satomi: How much will that cost?

Chris: About $30. But you might add a tip for the taxi driver. That's my advice— almost everyone tips. We usually tip about 15 percent.

Satomi: I see. What about money? What's the best way to keep my money?

Chris: Well, you could use traveler's checks, or you must open a bank account.

Using Modals and Phrasal Modals of Necessity and Prohibition

Complete the paragraph using modals and phrasal modals of necessity and prohibition.

Welcome to English 101. My name is Lisa Rosado, and I'll be your teacher.

Let me tell you a few things about the course. You _don't have to_ take notes right
1

now. Just listen carefully.

First, you _____ attend class regularly. If you want credit for this course,
2

you _____ miss more than six classes. You _____ come on time,
3 4

too.

You _____ complete all the homework assignments. For informal
5

assignments, handwriting is OK. You _____ type them. But you
6

_____ type formal assignments. And there are two exams. You
7

_____ pass these to pass the course.
8

You _____ have a dictionary for this class, but it's a very good idea.
9

Does anyone have any questions?

COMBINING FORM, MEANING, AND USE

7 **Thinking About Meaning and Use**

Choose the correct sentence to complete each conversation.

1. **A:** I'd like to learn how to dance.

   B: _____

   a. You must take some lessons.

   b. Maybe you should take some lessons.

2. **A:** Should I get some milk?

   B: _____ We still have enough.

   a. You don't need to.

   b. You must not.

3. **A:** I've got a bad sore throat and I feel terrible.

   B: _____

   a. You might go to bed early tonight.

   b. You'd better go to bed early tonight.

4. **A:** The car broke down on the way home.

   B: Not again! _____

       a. We could get a new car.

       b. We've got to get a new car.

5. **A:** What's a good way to lose weight?

   B: _____

       a. Well, you could join an exercise class.

       b. Well, you must not join an exercise class.

6. **A:** Can I come back for the blood test tomorrow morning?

   B: Yes. _____

       a. But you must not eat for 12 hours before the test.

       b. But you don't have to eat for 12 hours before the test.

8 **Writing**

On a separate sheet of paper, use the information below to write a one-paragraph letter. Give Bob your advice. Should he finish college now? Or should he take a year off? Use modals of advice and necessity in affirmative and negative statements.

Your friend Bob is thinking about dropping out of college. He has only one more year before he gets his degree, but he is bored with his classes. He wants to take a year off and then go back and finish his degree. However, his parents have told him that they won't pay for him to go back to college if he drops out now. He will have to pay for his own education.

> Dear Bob,
>
>   I really think that you should stay in school until you get your degree. You've got to think about your future....

Chapters 9–11

A. Choose the correct clause to complete each sentence.

1. I can't go out for dinner ____.
   a. because it's a special occasion
   b. because I don't have any money

2. I'd better go out for dinner ____.
   a. because there isn't any food at home
   b. because I'm on a diet

3. I'd better not go out for dinner ____.
   a. because it's expensive
   b. because it's a special occasion

4. I'd like to go out for dinner ____.
   a. because it's expensive
   b. because it's a special occasion

5. I don't have to go out for dinner ____.
   a. if I don't want to
   b. because I'm on a diet

6. I'd rather go out for dinner ____.
   a. because it's expensive
   b. because I don't cook well

B. Rewrite these sentences, making them negative. Use contractions when possible.

7. It might rain.

_____

8. I'd like to be in his situation.

_____

9. He has to do it.

_____

10. We'd better go now.

_____

11. They'd prefer to wait.

_____

12. She should leave.

_____

13. He may come.

_____

C. Find and correct the errors in these sentences.

14. It's really late. We really should to go home.

15. You don't have got to worry about dinner. Rosa has agreed to cook.

16. Yesterday I could run a mile in less than six minutes.

17. They would not rather work late tonight.

18. Where would you like go to college?

19. It's a long way to the station. I'd prefer to drive rather walk.

20. Susan might helps with our math homework.

21. When we lived in Africa, we can see elephants and giraffes.

D. Choose *two* words or phrases to complete each sentence.

22. _____ you give me a hand?

   a. Can   **b.** Could   **c.** May

23. Take an umbrella. It _____ rain later.

   a. can   **b.** could   **c.** might

24. Sorry I'm late. I _____ find a parking space.

   a. couldn't   **b.** may not   **c.** wasn't able to

25. I don't know where she is. She _____ be at work.

   a. can   **b.** may   **c.** might

26. My parents are probably getting worried now. I _____ go home.

   a. 'd better   **b.** could   **c.** should

27. If I don't wear my glasses, I _____ see the screen.

   a. can't   **b.** won't be able to   **c.** wouldn't

28. You _____ leave the room until the examination is over.

   a. can't   **b.** couldn't   **c.** may not

29. I can't vote because I'm 17, and you _____ be 18 before you can vote in this country.

   a. must   **b.** have to   **c.** ought to

30. That intersection is dangerous. They _____ put up a stop sign.

   a. can   **b.** ought to   **c.** should

12 Tag Questions

FORM

1 **Examining Form**

Read these statements with tag questions. Then read the situations, and complete the tasks below.

STATEMENTS

a. "You won't tell anyone about this, <u>will you</u>?"

b. "It's beautiful, isn't it?"

c. "You *do* know the way, don't you?"

d. "She looks just like her father, doesn't she?"

e. "It's warm in here, isn't it?"

f. "You couldn't help me with this, could you?"

SITUATIONS

_b_ 1. Two people are standing on the top of a mountain and admiring the view.

_____ 2. A man and a woman are standing on a corner looking at a street map.

_____ 3. A man is carrying a large, heavy box. His friend is walking next to him.

_____ 4. Two children are standing next to a broken vase.

_____ 5. Two women are working out in a gym.

_____ 6. A woman is talking to a mother and her baby.

---

1. Match the letter of each statement to the appropriate situation. The first one has been done for you.

2. Underline each tag. The first one has been done for you.

3. What kind of statements have negative tags? _____

4. What kind of statements have positive tags? _____

Working on Tag Questions

Complete these sentences with the correct tag questions.

1. You're leaving today, _aren't you_?

2. She has two brothers, _____?

3. It won't take long, _____?

4. I'm really silly, _____?

5. You don't like him much, _____?

6. He's been here before, _____?

7. It's a beautiful day, _____?

8. He can't speak Italian, _____?

3 **Writing Short Answers to Tag Questions**

Complete these conversations with the correct short answers.

1. **Josh:** It isn't raining, is it?

   Steve: _No, it isn't_. The sun is out.

2. **Maria:** You know Carl, don't you?

   Luisa: _____. We met last year.

3. **Paulo:** We're late, aren't we?

   Reiko: _____. But that's OK.

4. **Myles:** You haven't been waiting long, have you?

   Jada: _____. I just got here.

5. **Alex:** They liked the play, didn't they?

   Greg: _____. They thought it was great.

6. **Stefan:** You'll be on time, won't you?

   Ana: _____. I'm never late.

7. **Robin:** They don't live here, do they?

   Carl: _____. But they'd like to.

8. **Miguel:** I'm driving us to the airport tomorrow, aren't I?

   Silvio: _____. My car is being repaired.

MEANING AND USE

4) Understanding Tag Questions and *Yes/No* Questions

Choose the better question for each situation.

1. You're sitting next to someone on a plane. He just finished speaking with someone else in a foreign language. You want to say something to him, but you haven't heard him speak English. You say:

   a. Do you speak English?

   b. You speak English, don't you?

2. You're standing next to a stranger at a bus stop. It's very cold for this time of year. You say:

   a. It's cold today, isn't it?

   b. Is it cold today?

3. You leave your house with a friend and go toward the car. You realize that you didn't lock the front door of the house. You say to your friend:

   a. Did I lock the front door?

   b. I didn't lock the front door, did I?

4. You're going to a picnic that your company is giving. You work with Maria. You don't know if she is going to the picnic or not. You ask her:

   a. Will you be at the picnic?

   b. You won't be at the picnic, will you?

5) Making Polite Requests

Rewrite these sentences as polite requests with tag questions.

1. Could you lend me your car?

   You couldn't lend me your car, could you?

2. Do you have an extra pen?

   _____

3. Could you wait until tomorrow?

   _____

4. Would you be able to work late today?

   _____

5. Could you come here a little earlier?

   _____

6. Do you know what time it is?

   _____

Read the conversations and complete the task below.

Conversation 1 (Megan and Fumiko are at home.)

Megan: I'm going to do some errands.
Fumiko: You couldn't mail these letters for me, could you?

Conversation 2 (Eva and Rosa are standing in front of a school.)

Eva: You look familiar.
Rosa: You look familiar, too. . . . You're Elena's mother, aren't you?

Conversation 3 (Carlos and Hanna are sitting on a park bench in spring.)

Carlos: It's a beautiful day!
Hanna: Yes. The weather has been great, hasn't it?

Conversation 4 (Yuji and Rick are at the train station.)

Yuji: Can I help you?

Rick: A ticket to Centerville, please. I just have the schedule for last year. The trains still go every hour on the hour, don't they?

Write the number of the conversation in which the speaker uses a tag question to:

1. ask for agreement: _3_   3. make a polite request: _____

2. confirm information: _____, _____

COMBINING FORM, MEANING, AND USE

Read this conversation. There are several places where tag questions would be appropriate. Add tags to statements in the conversation to make five more tag questions.

Amy: That was a lovely ceremony, *wasn't it?*
                                       ∧

Sara: Yes, it was.

Amy: My name is Amy. We've never met before.

Sara: No. I'm Sara. It's nice to meet you.

Amy: Lauren looks beautiful.

Sara: Uh-huh. How do you know Lauren?

Amy: We went to school together. And you're a friend of Tony's.

Sara: That's right. We work together.

Amy: You and he work at Intellek.

Sara: Yeah. Oh, look. That's Lauren's father. Let's go say hello.

On a separate sheet of paper, write a short conversation for each of the situations shown below. In each conversation, include statements with tag questions and short answers.

A: It's a beautiful view, isn't it?

B: Yes, it is.

13 Additions with Conjunctions

FORM

1 **Examining Form**

Read this article and complete the tasks below.

Twin Coincidences?

Identical twins Julie and Lisa have a number of things in common besides a birthday. They both work in education: Julie is a teacher, and Lisa

5 is a counselor. <u>Julie has two children, and so does Lisa.</u> Lisa is married to a man named Mark; Julie's husband is Matt. Even their husbands look alike. Mark is tall and fair, and so is

10 Matt. Both men are lawyers.

As children, the girls were both very good at sports. But Lisa couldn't do math, and neither could Julie. In fact, Lisa failed math in ninth grade,

15 and Julie did too.

The coincidences have continued in adulthood. Lisa had a boy and then a girl, and so did Julie. When Lisa was having her first baby, Julie had

20 such a stomachache that she could not get up. Then, six months later, Lisa woke in the night with a fright. She called Julie immediately and found out that Julie had been in a car

25 accident and had a broken leg.

Lisa can't explain any of this, and Julie can't either. It's all part of the mystery of being a twin.

1. There are six examples of sentences with *and so, and . . . too, and . . . either,* or *and neither.* The first one is underlined. Underline five more.

2. What kind of sentences does *and . . . so* connect, affirmative or negative?

_____

Complete these sentences with *and, but, too,* or *either.*

1. I live in Chicago, <u>and</u> my sister does <u>too</u>.

2. I don't speak Chinese, _____ my parents don't _____.

3. My mother works, _____ my father does _____.

4. My father is a doctor, _____ my sister is _____.

5. I live at home, _____ my sister doesn't.

6. I'm not good at sports, _____ my sister isn't _____.

7. We've been to Europe, _____ our parents haven't.

8. I don't like loud music, _____ my parents don't _____.

9. I enjoy math, _____ I certainly don't enjoy biology.

10. My brother plays tennis, _____ I play tennis _____.

3 Completing Sentences

Complete this story. You may use *so, too, either,* or *neither.* You may also use a form of *be, do,* or a modal.

I met my friend Lee when we were both waiting to see a movie. I love old movies,
and Lee <u>does</u> too. One evening I was waiting in line to see *Psycho,* and
_____ was Lee. We started talking. I said that I didn't want to wait in line,
and Lee said he didn't _____. So we went to have coffee.

As we were talking, we found that we have similar backgrounds. He comes
from a big family, and I _____ too. He went to college in Boston, and
so _____ I. He didn't graduate, and _____ did I. He's spent
time in South America, and I _____ too. I speak Spanish, but Lee
_____.

Lee and I have known each other for five years now. He often comes over for dinner.
He lives alone, and I do _____. I can cook well, but Lee _____.
Also, I like to cook, but he _____. I like to cook good, healthy food. I'm a
health nut, but Lee certainly _____!

MEANING AND USE

Using Responses

Complete these conversations with responses that use *so* or *neither*.

1. **Lee:** I like most movies.

   John: _So do I._

2. **Betty:** I loved *Gone with the Wind*.

   Rosa: _____

3. **Victor:** I don't like horror movies very much.

   Larry: _____

4. **Eric:** I didn't like that movie at all.

   Hector: _____

5. **Andre:** I sometimes watch old movies on TV.

   Nicole: _____

6. **Keiko:** I can't stand long movies.

   Satomi: _____

Expressing Similarities

Rewrite these sentences, using the words in parentheses. Make all necessary changes.

1. Sharks live in the ocean, and so do whales. (too)

   Sharks live in the ocean, and whales do too.

2. Cats are popular pets, and dogs are too. (so)

   _____

3. Kangaroos are not native to the U.S., and neither are koalas. (either)

   _____

4. Kangaroos come from Australia, and so do koalas. (too)

   _____

5. Tigers don't live in groups, and leopards don't either. (neither)

   _____

6. Lions have killed people, and tigers have too. (so)

   _____

COMBINING FORM, MEANING, AND USE

6) Thinking About Meaning and Use

Look at the following chart that compares three children. Write a sentence for each of the phrases. More than one answer may be possible. Use *and ... too, and ... either, and so, and neither,* and *but.*

	KEVIN	CHRIS	BEN
1. wears glasses	✓	✓	
2. doesn't have brothers or sisters			✓
3. has been to Disneyland		✓	✓
4. went to preschool	✓		
5. can read a little	✓		✓
6. can't swim		✓	
7. doesn't like spinach	✓	✓	
8. would like a bike for his birthday	✓		✓

1. _Kevin and Chris wear glasses, but Ben doesn't._

   OR Kevin wears glasses, and so does Chris.

   OR Kevin wears glasses, and Chris does too.

2. _____

3. _____

4. _____

5. _____

6. _____

7. _____

8. _____

Read this online dating page and complete the task below.

NAME	JAKE	DEREK
Singles of the Month *Meet October's singles of the month!* If you would like to meet any of these people, send an e-mail to: Singles@singlesofthemonth.com		
Age	21	23
Occupation	student	computer graphics designer
From	Houston, Texas	San Jose, California
Free time	goes to the gym, plays video games, surfs the Internet	goes to movies, listens to classical music, goes to concerts, runs
Likes	camping, hiking, the outdoors, dogs, hip-hop music	classical music, reading the Sunday newspaper, shopping
Dislikes	shopping for clothes, exams	heavy metal music, cleaning the house
NAME	HOLLY	KIM
Age	25	23
Occupation	part-time student	software engineer
From	Austin, Texas	Sunnyvale, California
Free time	studies, listens to music, runs	goes to movies, goes to the gym, chats on the Internet
Likes	long hikes, camping, all kinds of music	traveling, shopping, cooking, her cat
Dislikes	housework, writing papers	loud music

Imagine you are looking for a partner. On a separate sheet of paper, write an e-mail to one of the singles. Tell what you have in common with him or her. Compare your likes and dislikes. Use *and . . . too, and . . . either, and so, and neither,* and *but.*

Dear Jake,

    I saw your ad on Singles of the Month. We like a lot of the same things! You like camping and hip-hop, and I do, too. . . .

Chapters 12–13

A. Complete each sentence with one word.

1. I'm from Texas, and so _____ they.

2. I'm not interested, and _____ is my husband.

3. She's a lawyer, and so _____ he.

4. I'd like that, and you _____ too.

5. I can't speak Spanish, but my parents _____.

6. My father works and my mother does _____.

7. Robert works hard, and _____ does Elaine.

8. She'll be early, but he _____.

9. My mom loves chocolate, and so _____ my dad.

B. Write a tag question for each of these sentences.

10. She plays very well, _____?

11. That wasn't a joke, _____?

12. They've been here before, _____?

13. You don't have the time, _____?

14. That's a nice painting, _____?

15. You have three sisters, _____?

16. They weren't waiting long, _____?

17. I'm late again, _____?

18. You haven't seen this movie, _____?

19. You went shopping, _____?

20. You couldn't help me, _____?

21. Sandra can drive, _____?

C. Match the questions in Column 1 with the responses in Column 2.

Column 1

_____ **22.** It's not raining, is it?

_____ **23.** You don't really mean that, do you?

_____ **24.** That was a great meal, wasn't it?

_____ **25.** You've met Andrea, haven't you?

_____ **26.** This won't hurt, will it?

Column 2

a. Yes, it was fantastic.

b. Yes, I have.

c. No, I don't. I was joking.

d. You won't feel a thing.

e. No! The sun is out.

D. Complete this conversation with the appropriate words.

A: I don't like flying.

B: _____ do I. I don't fly very often.
  27

A: I don't _____. Do you live in San Francisco?
  28

B: Yes. I just moved there last year.

A: I _____, too. What part?
  29

B: The Richmond.

A: What a coincidence! I live there _____.
  30

14 Nouns and Quantity Expressions

FORM

1 Examining Form

Read this newspaper article and complete the tasks below.

Question of the Week

How Do You Deal with Money?

"I'm terrible with money. I spend my paycheck as soon as I get it. This means I often don't have much cash at the end of the month, and I have to borrow a
5 few dollars from my boyfriend. He doesn't like that."
Donna, 27, North Carolina

"We need to learn how to do better. My husband earns a good salary, but
10 we also have many expenses. We have a big house and several cars, and we spend a great deal of money on travel. We need to save because we're going to retire soon."
15 ***Sun-hee, 58, Illinois***

"I guess I deal with it pretty well. I never have any problems with money. I work a lot of hours, so I usually don't have much time to shop. Also, there
20 aren't many things I need."
Pedro, 32, California

"Sorry–I can't give you much information on that topic. I'm a student, and my parents deal with the
25 money. Right now I have no job because they want me to concentrate on my studies. But this summer I'm going to do some work for my dad, for good pay, so ask me again then."
30 ***Greg, 17, Arkansas***

---

1. There are twelve examples of general quantity expressions in the newspaper article. The first one is underlined. Underline eleven more.

2. Find the count and noncount nouns that go with each quantity expression. Circle the count nouns and put a box around the noncount nouns. The first one is done for you.

Working on Quantity Expressions

Choose the correct quantity expression to complete each sentence.

1. The mayor has _____ friends.
   a. a great deal of
   b. a lot of

2. I'll take _____ sugar in my coffee.
   a. a teaspoon
   b. a teaspoon of

3. We haven't heard _____ news lately.
   a. much
   b. many

4. There were _____ children at the party.
   a. several
   b. a great deal of

5. We had _____ rain last night, didn't we?
   a. many
   b. a lot of

6. _____ people came to the meeting yesterday.
   a. A few
   b. A little

7. _____ oranges did you buy?
   a. How much
   b. How many

8. Some plants need _____ water.
   a. little
   b. few

MEANING AND USE

3 **Using Specific Quantity Expressions**

Choose the correct quantity expression from the box to complete each sentence.

box	can	cup	jar	pile
bunch	carton	drop	slice	bag

1. We need a _box_ of cereal.

2. You'll need about a _____ of sugar to make a cake.

3. Please buy a _____ of soup.

4. The cheesecake is wonderful here. It's only $2.00 a _____.

5. We haven't had a _____ of rain all summer.

6. What a beautiful _____ of flowers!

7. Get me a _____ of eggs.

8. I'll get a _____ of mayonnaise.

9. I will bring a _____ of potato chips for the party.

10. We watched the children play in the large _____ of leaves.

Read the information below. Then choose the correct quantity expression to complete the descriptions that follow.

A.

Washington High School 12th Grade Student Participation in Music Classes	
Instrument	**Number of Students**
guitar	32
piano	25
drums	6
flute	4
saxophone	4
clarinet	4
violin	2
Total Music Students	**77**
Total Students	**105**

A lot of ____ (A lot of/Several) students take music classes in 12th grade.
1

_____ (A few/A lot of) kids play guitar. _____ (Few/Quite a
2   3

few) students play piano. _____ (Some/Many) students play the
4

saxophone or the clarinet. _____ (Very few/Quite a few) students play
5

the violin. This year there are _____ (no/some) trumpet players.
6

B.

How Americans Spend Time at Home: Average Hours Per Person Per Year	
Activity	**Hours**
watching TV	1,650
listening to the radio	1,047
listening to music	357
reading books and newspapers	265
writing letters	28

Americans spend _____ (a great deal of/some) time in front of the
1

television and _____ (quite a lot of/very little) time listening to the
2

radio. They also spend _____ (very little/some) time listening to music
3

and reading books and newspapers, but they spend _____ (very
4

little/some) time writing letters.

A. Rewrite these sentences, replacing the word *homework* with *assignments*. Make any other changes as necessary.

1. There isn't much homework this year.

   There aren't many assignments this year.

2. Here's some homework for you.

   _____

3. There's a lot of homework for this class.

   _____

4. She gives very little homework.

   _____

5. We don't have any homework tonight.

   _____

6. Please don't give us so much homework.

   _____

B. Rewrite these sentences, replacing the word *jobs* with *work*. Make any other changes as necessary.

1. I have a few jobs for you.

   I have a little work for you.

2. There are no jobs in this town.

   _____

3. How many jobs are available?

   _____

4. There aren't many interesting jobs.

   _____

5. These are essential jobs.

   _____

6. There are very few jobs here.

   _____

COMBINING FORM, MEANING, AND USE

A. Complete these questions with *How much* or *How many.*

1. <u>How many</u> close friends do you have?

2. _____ money do you spend on clothes?

3. _____ TV do you watch?

4. _____ pairs of shoes do you have?

5. _____ water do you drink every day?

6. _____ time do you spend in the shower?

7. _____ countries have you visited?

8. _____ cousins do you have?

B. Answer the questions in part A using general quantity expressions.

1. _____   5. _____

2. _____   6. _____

3. _____   7. _____

4. _____   8. _____

7 **Writing**

On a separate sheet of paper, write a paragraph explaining how you make something that you like to eat. If you don't cook, describe how you make a favorite sandwich or drink. Use general and specific quantity expressions.

> I love peanut butter and jelly sandwiches, and I have my own way of making them. First, I take a slice of bread and cover it with a lot of peanut butter—the kind that has a lot of chunks of peanuts in it. Then I put a little jelly on the top—but not too much! . . .

Indefinite and Definite Articles

FORM

Read this article and complete the tasks below.

"Christina's World" is ⓐ painting by an American artist, Andrew Wyeth. It is probably his most famous painting.

5 In the painting, a young woman is sitting or lying in an open field. It is around noon, and the sun is shining. The woman is looking toward a group of buildings on a farm. The buildings are far away. Her back is toward the 10 viewer, and her body stretches at an angle across the painting. Her position is one of the things that make this such an interesting painting.

The painting creates different feelings in different viewers. Many people feel loneliness or sadness. Others feel hope. The hopefulness may come from the idea that the woman will not have to stay in the world we see in the painting. 15 She will have the courage to escape someday and find a place of her own.

1. There are many examples of definite and indefinite articles in the article. Circle all the indefinite articles (*a, an*). Underline all the definite articles (*the*). The first one is done for you.

2. Find two examples of each of the following. If an adjective is included, write the adjective, too.

   a. *a/an* + singular count noun: _a painting_

   b. *the* + singular count noun: _____

   c. *the* + noncount noun: _____

   d. *the* + plural count noun: _____

   e. noncount noun with no article: _____

Working on *A/An*

Complete these phrases with *a* or *an*.

1. _an_ exercise program

2. _____ university professor

3. _____ unusual event

4. _____ one-way street

5. _____ honest man

6. _____ hospital bed

7. _____ only child

8. _____ early start

9. _____ hourly rate

10. _____ unique experience

Choosing Indefinite or Definite Articles

Complete these conversations with *a/an* or *the*.

Conversation 1

Gina: Hurry up! You'll miss _the_ bus!
₁

Rick: Mom, I need _____ dollar for lunch.
₂

Gina: Don't you have _____ lunch I packed?
₃

Rick: No, I don't. I'd rather get _____ hamburger at school.
₄

Conversation 2

Eric: I'm going to _____ store. Do we need anything?
₁

Kedra: Yes, we need _____ carton of milk.
₂

Eric: What about _____ milk in the refrigerator?
₃

Kedra: There isn't enough. By the way, _____ car needs gas.
₄

Conversation 3

Lisa: I'm hungry. Can I have _____ cookie?
₁

Juan: _____ cookies are for later. Have _____ apple.
₂ ₃

Lisa: I don't like apples. I'd like _____ banana.
₄

Juan: OK. There's _____ banana in _____ refrigerator.
₅ ₆

MEANING AND USE

Using *The*

Read the conversations and complete the task below.

1. **Julie:** What's Mark doing?
   Lisa: He's talking on the phone.

2. **Rita:** Where are you going?
   Won-joon: To the park.

3. **Dan:** I'm reading an interesting book.
   Miguel: What's the book about?

4. **Keiko:** When are you graduating?
   Carol: The semester after next.

5. **Luisa:** Do you think there is life on the moon?
   Alex: I don't know. Maybe.

6. **Sasha:** It sounds like they're having a party.
   Jenny: Yeah. The music is really loud.

Identify the conversations where the speaker uses *the* because the noun:

1. is something familiar to the speaker and listener in daily life. <u>1,</u>_____

2. is identified by further information in the sentence. _____

3. was already mentioned. _____

4. is something the speaker and listener can see or hear. _____

5. is something unique (there is only one of them). _____

Understanding Indefinite and Definite Articles

Complete the joke with *a/an* or *the*.

   <u>A</u>   man who was very upset went to see _____ doctor. "Doctor, I have
    1   2

_____ problem. You have to help me!" he cried.
   3

"What's _____ problem?" asked _____ doctor.
          4   5

"I keep having _____ dream. In this dream, there's _____ door with
                      6   7

_____ sign on it. I push and push and push _____ door, but I can't open it."
  8   9

"What does _____ sign say?" asked _____ doctor.
               10   11

"Pull," said _____ patient.
            12

A. Read the sayings in the chart, and think about what they mean. What is your opinion of each one? Check (✓) the appropriate column.

	I AGREE.	I DISAGREE.	I'M NOT SURE.
1. Life is sweet.			
2. The early bird catches the worm.			
3. A leopard can't change its spots.			
4. Beggars can't be choosers.			
5. The pen is mightier (stronger) than the sword.			
6. Time flies.			
7. Bad news travels fast.			
8. A friend to all is a friend to none.			
9. Love is blind.			
10. Children should be seen but not heard.			

B. Look at how the subject nouns in the sayings in part A are used to make general statements. Then complete these tasks.

1. Find four examples of a noncount noun without an article.

   <u>life</u>

2. Find two examples of a plural count noun without an article.

   _____

3. Find two examples of indefinite article + singular count noun.

   _____

4. Find two examples of definite article + singular count noun.

   _____

COMBINING FORM, MEANING, AND USE

7) Editing

There are thirteen errors in this student's composition. The first one has been corrected. Correct twelve more.

~~The~~ computers have become important in the business and in everyday life. In my life as student, computers help me in a couple of ways.

First, computers help me communicate with people. Every day I check my e-mail. I often have the messages from my family or from a friend. E-mail saves me a lot of the time and money. I don't have to wait for letters or stand in line at post office to buy the stamps. At university where I study, students can communicate with their teachers by e-mail. I sometimes use e-mail to send assignment.

Second, my computer helps me prepare my assignments. If I have the paper to write, I can search the Internet to get an information. The word-processing program on computer makes it easy to write many drafts. The program checks grammar and spelling. When I make the mistakes, the program marks them so I can find and correct them.

8) Writing

Which of these three items do you think is the most useful for most people: a cell phone, a portable CD player, or a laptop computer? On a separate sheet of paper, write a paragraph saying why and how the item is useful. Support your ideas with specific examples.

I think a portable CD player is the most useful item for most people. People can take a CD player with them everywhere. For example, I sometimes take one with me when I go to the gym. . . .

Chapters 14–15

A. Circle the noncount noun in each set of words.

1. chair/furniture/table

2. postcard/mail/letter

3. work/job/task

4. event/luck/accident

5. prison/freedom/prisoner

6. suitcase/bag/baggage

7. hint/tip/advice

8. car/gas/road

9. ring/jewelry/necklace

10. money/coin/check

11. information/fact/opinion

12. report/news/article

B. Find and correct the errors in these sentences.

13. The living room is nicest room in our house.

14. It's a small room, and it's next to kitchen.

15. There's a red rug on the floor and large, comfortable sofa to sit on.

16. Across room from the sofa are two armchairs.

17. We have lot of family pictures on the walls.

18. There's the large plant next to the window.

19. The window has the white curtains.

20. I like a living room because I spend time there with my family.

21. Whenever a special shows are on TV, we eat our dinner there.

22. I like to watch TV and eat at a same time.

23. When we have a guests, they sleep on the sofa in the living room.

24. Sometimes I fall asleep in living room while watching TV.

C. Choose *two* words or phrases to complete each sentence.

25. **A:** Where is your furniture?

    B: I gave _____ to my brother.

    a. it   **b.** some   **c.** them

26. I think you should hire Wendy. She has _____ experience.

    a. a lot of   **b.** many   **c.** some

27. There are _____ good books on this subject.

    a. a lot of   **b.** several   **c.** a great deal of

28. You're bored! You need to have _____ fun.

    a. a little   **b.** little   **c.** some

29. I'm going out with _____ friends.

    a. a few   **b.** few   **c.** some

30. Why don't we invite Nicole? She doesn't have _____ friends yet.

    a. much   **b.** any   **c.** many

CHAPTER

16 Adjectives

FORM

1 **Examining Form**

Read this gossip column and complete the task below.

Talk of the Town

Everybody important is getting ready for next Wednesday's dinner at the Concert House. The famous writer Susan Stravinsky will be at this special event. She

5 plans to wear an elegant black wool dress by designer Claude Brache.

Actress Trudy Koh is shopping for something unusual to wear. It's her birthday next week: She'll be twenty-four

10 years old. Trudy and her boyfriend, Sam Hamilton, spent a relaxing weekend in Easthampton. While they were there, they gave a dinner for artist Raoul Solvenberg. Everyone says the food was excellent. The

15 menu included lamb with creamed red potatoes and fresh local corn. Joe Gardner, the actor (and Trudy's previous boyfriend), was a guest at the dinner–and Joe seemed very happy to be there.

20 Finally, supermodel Lili Andersen was in town last week to show her new creams for the face and body. The creams are based on an ancient Indian formula that Lili discovered on her recent trip to

25 South Asia. At Mackie's Department Store on Tuesday, Lili looked beautiful in a pink silk sleeveless dress and white straw hat.

Look back at the gossip column. Find the adjectives that modify the nouns in the chart. Some nouns have more than one adjective. Which adjectives follow stative verbs?

NOUN	LINE	MODIFIER(S)	NOUN	LINE	MODIFIER(S)
1. everybody	1	important	**9.** corn	16	
2. writer	3		**10.** boyfriend	17	
3. event	4		**11.** Joe	18	
4. dress	5		**12.** creams	21	
5. something	8		**13.** formula	23	
6. weekend	11		**14.** Lili	26	
7. food	14		**15.** dress	27	
8. potatoes	16		**16.** hat	28	

Adjectives   91

Form an adjective from the underlined noun in each sentence. Use the endings in parentheses.

A. (-*ful*)

   1. Politicians have a lot of <u>power</u>. They're _powerful_ people.

   2. I have a <u>pain</u> in my leg. It's quite _____.

   3. There is a lot of <u>stress</u> in your job. It's very _____ work.

   4. I'd like to have <u>success</u> in business. I'd like to be a _____ businessperson.

B. (-*less*)

   1. I don't see the <u>point</u> of this homework. It seems _____.

   2. Ben never does things with <u>care</u>. He's quite a _____ person.

   3. That old man doesn't have a <u>home</u>. He's _____.

   4. I don't have much <u>hope</u> we'll get the loan. The situation looks pretty _____.

C. (-*able*)

   1. The designers of that car really thought about <u>comfort</u>. It's a very _____ car.

   2. The expert has a lot of <u>knowledge</u>. He's very _____.

   3. The <u>value</u> of this camera is over $1,000. It's a _____ camera.

   4. Bob is making a good <u>profit</u> from his bookstore. It's a _____ bookstore.

D. (-*y*)

   1. It is very pleasant to sit in the <u>shade</u>. Move your chair under this _____ tree.

   2. The tools are covered with <u>rust</u>. They are very _____.

   3. Add <u>salt</u> to the soup. However, make sure it's not too _____.

   4. There was a lot of <u>dirt</u> on the floor. The windows were also very _____.

E. (-*ic*)

   1. The mayor said that the fireman was a <u>hero</u>. His actions were _____.

   2. He writes like a real <u>poet</u>. His letters are very _____.

   3. To succeed in this job, you need to act like a <u>diplomat</u>. You have to be very _____.

   4. He's a professional <u>athlete</u>. His brother is also very _____.

Working on Placement of Adjectives

Use the words below to make sentences. Some sentences can be written in more than one way. Punctuate your sentences correctly.

1. tired / man / old / looked / the

   <u>The old man looked tired.</u>

2. actor / tall / the / and / was / handsome / dark

   _____

3. man / rich / is / previous / boss / my / a

   _____

4. anything / didn't / I / special / buy

   _____

5. tree / over / thirty / this / is / old / years

   _____

6. tiring / had / we / trip / a / difficult

   _____

MEANING AND USE

Understanding the Order of Adjectives

Rewrite these sentences, adding the adjectives in parentheses. Be careful about the order of the adjectives. Make any necessary changes.

1. She was wearing pants. (blue/fishing/heavy)

   <u>She was wearing heavy blue fishing pants.</u>

2. They have a table. (beautiful/dining room/wooden)

   _____

3. Enjoy a glass of water. (delicious/mineral)

   _____

4. I'm going to wear my shoes. (running/comfortable/old)

   _____

5. I love my typewriter. (black/old)

   _____

6. He has a car. (expensive/new)

   _____

Choose the best adjective from the box to complete each sentence.

amazed	amazing
annoyed	annoying
bored	boring
embarrassed	embarrassing
excited	exciting
interested	interesting
terrified	terrifying
tired	tiring

1. Celia is getting a degree in archaeology. She's always been _interested_ in ancient history.

2. When I felt the earthquake, I thought, "This is it. I'm going to die." I was _____ .

3. I can't be late to class. The teacher gets really _____ when people come in late.

4. I don't want to go to that class. The professor is so _____ that I fall asleep in my seat.

5. I ran into an old friend the other day, and I couldn't remember his name. It was so _____! I didn't know what to say.

6. Long plane trips are pretty _____. You always miss sleep when you cross time zones.

7. When I woke up and looked at the clock, I was _____ to find that I had slept for 12 hours.

8. Sorry about the noise. The kids are all _____ because they're going to the zoo this afternoon.

COMBINING FORM, MEANING, AND USE

6 Thinking About Meaning and Use

Look at this picture and use adjectives to complete the description below.

I saw a(n) <u>unusual</u> woman yesterday. She had _____
1   2
_____ hair. She was wearing a(n) _____ jacket, a(n)
3   4
_____ _____ sweater, and a(n) _____ skirt. Her
5   6   7
boots were _____ and had _____ heels. She looked really
8   9

_____ .
10

7 Writing

On a separate sheet of paper, write a paragraph describing an unusual-looking person
that you know or that you have seen. You can describe the person as he/she looks
now, using present tenses. Or using past tenses, you can describe the person as he/she
looked at some time in the past. Use a variety of adjectives in your paragraph.

> My friend Emily looks very interesting and unusual. She
> is about thirty-five years old. She is tall and has beautiful
> eyes. . . .

17 Adverbs

FORM

Read this excerpt from a novel and complete the task below.

Chapter 4

Romance in the Raindrops

Margaret walked to the window and stood there silently for a long time. She stared at the raindrops that were moving slowly down the window. Umberto wondered what she was thinking. Finally, she turned and she looked at him quite sadly.

5   "I've been thinking about it all," she said very carefully, "and I've decided that I can't marry you."

Umberto rose to leave.

"Wait!" she cried desperately. "Sit down, Umberto, please. I must tell you why."

10   "But I know why," Umberto replied. "It's because of the money. The money that your father has promised if you marry Giorgio. The money that I cannot give you. The money…"

"No, Umberto," Margaret said quietly. "It's because of me." She began to cry.

Find and write the adverbs of manner that answer the questions below.

a. How did Margaret stand at the window? <u>silently</u>

b. How were the raindrops moving down the window? _____

c. How did Margaret look at Umberto? _____

d. How did Margaret speak? _____ _____ _____

Read these sentences. Is the underlined word an adverb or an adjective? Check (✓) the correct column.

	ADJECTIVE	ADVERB
1. We caught an <u>early</u> plane to Phoenix.	✓	
2. Let's get there <u>early</u>.		
3. Please don't drive <u>fast</u>.		
4. It's a <u>hard</u> decision to make.		
5. I'll <u>definitely</u> be there.		
6. Don't hit it <u>hard</u>. You'll break it.		
7. The neighbors are really <u>friendly</u>.		
8. Are you feeling <u>lonely</u>?		
9. They arrived <u>late</u> for dinner.		
10. I don't sing very <u>well</u>.		

3 **Forming Adverbs from Adjectives**

Rewrite each sentence, changing the underlined noun into a verb and changing the adjective into an adverb. Make any other necessary changes. Do not change the tense.

1. The woman's <u>disappearance</u> was mysterious.

   The woman disappeared mysteriously.

2. I feel tremendous <u>admiration</u> for Jake.

   _____

3. The President made a brief <u>appearance</u>.

   _____

4. Chris and Gina have constant <u>arguments</u>.

   _____

5. Marta's <u>writing</u> is very good.

   _____

6. She gave the children a loving <u>hug</u>.

   _____

Working on Placement of Adverbs

Rewrite these sentences, putting the adverbs in parentheses in the correct places.
More than one answer may be possible.

1. She ran to the phone and dialed. (quickly/nervously)

   She ran quickly to the phone and dialed nervously.

2. The hurricane hit the Florida coast. (hard)

   _____

3. We're going to move. (probably)

   _____

4. It's not raining. (definitely/hard)

   _____

5. You didn't like him. (obviously)

   _____

6. She speaks Spanish. (maybe/well)

   _____

7. He drove. (yesterday/carefully)

   _____

8. She dances. (beautifully/certainly)

   _____

Working on *So . . . That; Such (a). . . That*

Complete these sentences with *so, such,* or *such a* and an appropriate adjective.

1. The buildings are _so tall_____ that you can't see the sky.

2. That was _____ movie that I went to see it again.

3. The beach is _____ that we can walk to it.

4. We've had _____ weather that we haven't been able to go out.

5. The restaurant serves _____ portions that we can never finish
   our food.

6. This is _____ jacket that I don't notice the cold.

7. You gave me _____ advice last time that I'm asking you for
   advice again.

8. This computer is _____ that you can download material in seconds.

MEANING AND USE

Read this speech and complete the tasks below.

> "Hello, everybody. I'd just like to say how very happy I am to see you all here today.
>
> "First, I would like to thank Betty. She organized this event so well. Betty works quietly, so some of you might not realize how much work she does. I don't know what we'd do without her.
>
> "And I'd like to say how delighted I am to see Susan Beck back with us this year. As you know, Susan was ill recently but is now back at her desk and working hard. I think we all noticed that the orders are certainly moving smoothly now. So, thanks, Susan!
>
> "And now I have some good news. As you may know, sales have risen dramatically. If this continues, we will probably meet our sales goals soon, and we can confidently move forward into the new year. Obviously, you are the reason for our success. So I would like to thank all of you."

1. There are six adverbs that answer the question *How . . . ?* (adverbs of manner). Find the adverbs and the verbs they modify, and write them below.

ADVERB	VERB	ADVERB	VERB
a. <u>well</u>	a. <u>organized</u>	d. _____	d. _____
b. _____	b. _____	e. _____	e. _____
c. _____	c. _____	f. _____	f. _____

2. Find two adverbs that answer the question *When . . . ?* (adverbs of time).

   _____

3. Find one adverb that gives an opinion about a sentence (adverb of opinion).

   _____

4. Find two adverbs that show how sure the speaker is (adverbs of certainty).

   _____

7 Using *Too* and *Not Enough*

Rewrite these sentences in two different ways, using the words in parentheses and *too* or *not . . . enough* + an infinitive phrase. Do not change the meaning.

1. I'm not a teacher. I don't have any patience.

   (patient) I'm not patient enough to be a teacher.

   (impatient) I'm too impatient to be a teacher.

2. That suitcase won't hold all my clothes.

   (big) _____

   (small) _____

3. I can't watch that show because I don't get home in time.

   (late) _____

   (early) _____

4. That computer is very slow. It can't handle the job.

   (slow) _____

   (fast) _____

COMBINING FORM, MEANING, AND USE

8 Thinking About Meaning and Use

Choose the correct words to complete each conversation.

1. **A:** Did you buy the car?

   B: Yes, we did. _____
   - **a.** It wasn't too expensive.
   - **b.** It was too expensive.

2. **A:** Have you finished the report?

   B: No, but I want to. That's why

   _____
   - **a.** I'm hardly working on it.
   - **b.** I'm working hard on it.

3. **A:** How do you like your new apartment?

   B: I love it. _____
   - **a.** It's very big.
   - **b.** It's too big.

4. **A:** Is he going to Mexico this summer?

   B: I'm not sure. _____
   - **a.** He's definitely going.
   - **b.** Maybe he'll go.

5. **A:** Did you get a ride to the airport?

   B: Yes, but we got there _____.

   We missed the plane.
   - **a.** late
   - **b.** lately

6. **A:** Why aren't you wearing gloves?

   B: It's _____ to wear gloves.
   - **a.** warm enough
   - **b.** too warm

Using Adverbs in Writing

Read this story and complete the task below.

> Maria came into the room and sat down on the sofa. There was one other person there—a man. He was looking out the window and pulling his beard. The woman picked up a book and pretended to read it.
>
> Everything was quiet. A clock ticked on the mantelpiece. Some children were playing on the street outside. The man sighed.
>
> At 12 o'clock, the door opened and a woman looked in. "The dentist will see you now, Mrs. Harrison," she said.

Rewrite the story, adding adverbs to make it more interesting. Choose from the adverbs in the box or use your own ideas.

slowly	nervously	quietly	loudly
happily	obviously	suddenly	

Maria came into the room and sat down quietly on the sofa. . . .

_____

_____

_____

_____

_____

10 **Writing**

A. Look back at the story in Exercise 1. Think about the answers to these questions:

- Why can't Margaret marry Umberto?
- How does Umberto feel?
- Who is Giorgio?

B. On a separate sheet of paper, write the next part of the story. Try to include various kinds of adverbs—adverbs of manner, time, opinion, certainty, and degree.

Chapters 16–17

A. Find and correct the errors in these sentences.

   1. The children became terribly exciting when it started to snow.

   2. We can talk later. It's important nothing.

   3. You look hot and tiring. Do you want to sit down?

   4. I like your leather black boots. Are they new?

   5. Lorraine drives very slow.

   6. It was so a hot day that we decided to go for a nice, long swim in the lake.

   7. You don't exercise enough often. You should come to that new gym with me.

   8. I have visited recently Japan and Korea. It was a wonderful trip.

   9. Have you got enough money to buy the computer? It's extreme expensive.

  10. You need to work hardly if you want to do well in this class.

B. Rewrite these sentences, adding the words in parentheses. Make all the necessary changes. More than one order may be possible.

  11. Could I have some sparkling water? (mineral)

_____

  12. It's a Chinese custom. (traditional)

_____

  13. Your father will call tonight. (perhaps)

_____

  14. The princess was wearing a long evening dress. (black)

_____

  15. He doesn't want anything. (probably)

_____

  16. The officer examined my papers. (suspiciously)

_____

  17. Please don't do anything for my birthday. (special)

_____

18. We bought a lot of expensive equipment. (camping)

_____

19. They have some beautiful old furniture. (Italian)

_____

20. We are going away this summer. (definitely)

_____

C. Complete these sentences with the correct word or phrase.

21. Drive _____! The roads are icy.

    a. careful   **b.** carefully

22. He's not _____ tired to go out.

    a. enough   **b.** too

23. Mr. Parker was _____ teacher that everyone wanted to be in his class.

    a. a so good   **b.** such a good

24. I think archaeology is a _____ subject.

    a. fascinated   **b.** fascinating

25. Don't hit the window too _____ or the glass will break.

    a. hard   **b.** hardly

26. It's _____ to go out today. Let's wait until tomorrow.

    a. too wet   **b.** very wet

27. Ask Celia to sing. She sings _____.

    a. beautiful   **b.** beautifully

28. Tony is _____ good at math that he gets As in all his classes.

    a. so   **b.** such

29. We were all very _____ to hear your news.

    a. excited   **b.** exciting

30. You are all _____ good students that I'm not going to give you any homework.

    a. so   **b.** such

18 Comparatives

FORM

1 Examining Form

Read this article and complete the tasks below.

Rich in Cash, but Not in Happiness

We may deny it, but most of us secretly believe that people with more money are <u>happier</u>. We think that a higher salary, a more
5 expensive car, and a larger house in a better neighborhood will somehow bring happiness.

But is this true? Studies show that Americans have become richer
10 but not happier. For example, Americans' income increased by one-third from 1972 to 1991. Over the same period, the percentage of Americans saying they were "very
15 happy" actually decreased.

Why is this? Richard Easterlin, an economist at the University of Southern California, believes that we always compare our situations
20 with our neighbors'. When we feel we are doing better than our neighbors, we are satisfied. But when our neighbor buys a more beautiful home or a newer car, we
25 think we have to have those things, too. As a result, we never feel happy for very long.

We work harder in order to compete, and then we feel under
30 stress. Too much stress can actually shorten our lives. Economist Robert Frank says that Americans should use their wealth to live life more fully, to develop a more relaxed
35 lifestyle, and to spend more time with friends and family. He points out that people who don't have close social relationships tend to have more problems with health and to
40 die at a younger age.

---

1. There are eleven comparative adjectives in the article. The first one is underlined. Underline ten more.

2. Circle the three comparative adverbs.

3. Put a box around the comparative form of three nouns.

Write the comparative form of these adjectives and adverbs.

1. high _higher_

2. big _____

3. quickly _____

4. close _____

5. happy _____

6. softly _____

7. thin _____

8. healthy _____

9. well _____

10. satisfied _____

11. comfortable _____

12. bad _____

3 **Working on Comparative Adjectives and Adverbs**

Complete this story with the comparative form of the adjectives and adverbs in parentheses.

We are delighted with our new house, which is much _nicer_____
                                                                    1
(nice) than the old one. It's in a(n) _____ (attractive)
                                                2
neighborhood, and it's also _____ (conveniently) located because
                                         3
it's _____ (close) to both our jobs. I can leave work 15 minutes
          4
_____ (late) and arrive home at the same time as before. The
          5
other house was very dark; this one is _____ (sunny) because
                                                        6
it has _____ (big) windows and it faces south. So even though
             7
it's actually a little _____ (small) than the old one, it feels
                              8
_____ (spacious). The whole house is in _____
          9   10
(good) condition than the old one. The washer and other appliances are new and
run _____ (efficiently). The amazing thing is that the new house
          11
was even a little _____ (cheap)!
                         12

Completing Comparative Sentences

Complete each sentence with one word, either a verb or a pronoun. More than one answer may be possible.

1. My sister is older than <u>me/I</u>.

2. She's taller and prettier than I _____.

3. But I'm more intelligent than _____.

4. I work harder in school than she _____.

5. I got a higher TOEFL score than she _____.

6. I can run faster than she _____.

7. I'm a better athlete than she _____.

8. She has more friends than _____.

Working on *As . . . As*

Use the cues to write sentences with (*not*) *as . . . as*. Include a verb or an auxiliary at the end of the sentence when possible. More than one answer may be possible.

1. that child / eat / food / I

   <u>That child eats as much food as I do.</u>

2. my / brother / be not / old / I

   _____

3. you / speak / fluently / she

   _____

4. Amy / take / classes / he

   _____

5. they / be not / friendly / she

   _____

6. Kevin / work / hard / they

   _____

7. They / travel / we

   _____

8. Luisa / watch / TV / I

   _____

MEANING AND USE

6 **Using Comparatives with Nouns**

Rewrite these sentences, using the information given and the comparative forms of the nouns. More than one answer may be possible.

1. I don't have much time, but Myles does.

   I have <u>less time than Myles OR than Myles has</u>.

2. They have a lot of money, but we don't.

   They have _____.

3. There are only 16 math students and 25 foreign language students.

   There are _____ math students.

4. Stefan does a lot of work, but Holly doesn't.

   Holly does _____.

5. Read this article. It has a lot of information. The other one doesn't.

   This article has _____.

6. We own two TVs. The Smiths own four TVs.

   We own _____.

7 **Understanding (*Not*) As . . . As**

Rewrite these sentences, using the words in parentheses. Make other changes and add *not* as necessary. More than one answer may be possible.

1. She's taller than I am. (tall as)

   <u>I'm not as tall as her/she is.</u>

2. Biology isn't as difficult as physics. (easier)

   _____

3. I write better than Larry. (as well as)

   _____

4. Children aren't as polite as adults. (more polite)

   _____

5. The neighbor's dog barks more loudly than my dog. (as loudly as)

   _____

6. Morning traffic isn't as bad as evening traffic. (worse)

   _____

COMBINING FORM, MEANING, AND USE

8 **Expressing Differences with Comparatives and *Not As . . . As***

Write two answers to each question. Use comparative forms and *not as . . . as.*

What are the differences between . . .

1. a motorcycle and a scooter?

   A motorcycle is bigger than a scooter. A scooter is not as expensive
   as a motorcycle.

2. a coat and a raincoat?

3. a paperback book and a hardcover book?

4. an airplane and a helicopter?

9 **Writing**

A. Compare yourself with a brother or sister or with a close friend. Think about these questions:
   - Who is more popular? more outgoing? more confident?
   - Who is quieter? shyer?
   - Who is more traditional?
   - Who is more ambitious and hardworking?

Think about other differences and similarities and take some notes.

B. On a separate sheet of paper, write a paragraph comparing yourself to this person. Use comparatives and (*not*) *as . . . as* to express differences; use (*about/almost/nearly*) *as . . . as* to express similarities. Develop your ideas with examples. Do not use comparative forms in every sentence.

> My brother Mark is older than I am. He is quieter and
> more hardworking. He likes people, but I have more friends
> because he isn't as outgoing as I am. . . .

19 Superlatives

FORM

1 Examining Form

Read this magazine article and complete the tasks below.

Unusual Weather

The weather in the year from summer 1997 to summer 1998 was extremely unusual. In some parts of
5 the world, it was <u>the hottest</u> and the driest year on record. In other parts, it was the wettest year. That year everyone became aware of the weather pattern called "El Niño."
10   El Niño is part of a period of unusual weather that occurs every two to eight years. During El Niño, a pool of very warm water forms on the surface of the western Pacific. This
15 pool of warm water can disturb normal weather patterns around the world. By some measures, the 1997–1998 El Niño was the most powerful and the most destructive of
20 the twentieth century.
    Areas of the world that normally get very little rain, such as the coasts of southern Ecuador, Peru, and northern Chile, received large
25 amounts of rain. On the other hand, the tropical areas of Indonesia and northern Australia stayed dry during the period when the heaviest rain usually falls. In the United States, El
30 Niño also brought very hot and dry weather to Texas and Florida. For example, College Station, Texas, had the hottest weather in its history when the temperature stayed over
35 100 degrees Fahrenheit for 30 days in a row.

1. There are seven superlative forms in the article. The first one is underlined. Underline six more.

2. How are superlatives formed from one-syllable adjectives? _____

3. How are superlatives formed from most adjectives of two or more syllables?

_____

2 Forming Superlatives with Adjectives and Adverbs

Complete these sentences with the superlative form of the adjectives and adverbs in parentheses.

1. What was _the highest_ (high) score?

2. You really deserve a raise. Everyone here is a hard worker, but you work

   _____ (hard) of all.

3. She had _____ (unusual) costume at the party.

4. That is _____ (expensive) dish on the menu.

5. Who's been waiting _____ (long)?

6. This machine is _____ (fast) on the market right now.

7. We guarantee _____ (efficient) service.

8. Of my three brothers, Mark drives _____ (bad).

3 Working on Superlative Sentences

Rewrite these sentences as superlative sentences.

1. Young-soo is a good worker.

   Young-soo is the best worker.

2. He works hard.

   _____

3. He's very reliable.

   _____

4. He arrives early.

   _____

5. He does a lot of work.

   _____

6. He's popular with the customers.

   _____

7. He works carefully.

   _____

8. He's very friendly.

   _____

MEANING AND USE

4) Using Superlatives to Compare Members of a Group

Rewrite these sentences, using the superlative. Don't change meaning.

1. Derek and Eva have old cars, but mine is older.

   My car *is the oldest* _____.

2. My roommates have comfortable beds, but my bed is more comfortable.

   I _____.

3. My sisters swim well, but my brother swims better.

   My brother _____.

4. I have some time on Tuesday and Wednesday, but I don't have as much time on Thursday.

   I _____.

5. I have two children. My sister Megan has three children, and so does my brother Gary.

   I _____.

6. I drive fast. You drive fast. Carl drives even faster.

   Carl _____.

5) Giving Opinions with *One of* + Superlatives

Write sentences giving your opinions about the following things. Use *one of* + a superlative. End your sentences by indicating the group with an expression like *in the world/in the state, of all,* or *I've ever seen/I know.*

1. a beautiful city

   San Francisco is one of the most beautiful cities in the world.

2. a tall building

   _____

3. a dangerous sport

   _____

4. a good musician (or singer)

   _____

5. an important leader

   _____

COMBINING FORM, MEANING, AND USE

Use the information in the chart to complete the tasks below.

COUNTRY	AREA (SQUARE MILES)	COASTLINE (MILES)	NEIGHBORING COUNTRIES	POPULATION
Brazil	3,286,475	4,652	10	174,468,575
Canada	3,851,794	151,492	1	31,592,805
China	3,705,392	9,112	14	1,273,111,290

1. Write two superlative sentences about the size of the three countries in the group.

   Canada is the largest country.

   _____

2. Write two superlative sentences about the length of the coastlines of the three countries.

   _____

   _____

3. Write two superlative sentences about the number of neighbors that these three countries have.

   _____

   _____

4. Write two superlative sentences about the population of these three countries.

   _____

   _____

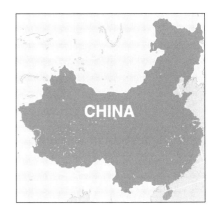

Editing

There are six superlative forms with errors in this paragraph. The first one has been corrected. Find and correct five more.

> We tested three car models: the Cheetah XS, the Onyx 2000, and the Zebra Deluxe. We agreed that, of the three, the Onyx gave us the smoothest and the ~~more~~ *most* comfortable ride. It was also the more quiet, even though it has the most powerful engine of the three. However, the Cheetah was most easiest to handle, and it performed the best at high speeds. At 50 miles per gallon, the Zebra was the most economical of the three models, but it was also the more expensive. All three cars were attractive, but we thought the Onyx was the beautifulest. Overall, we agreed that the most good buy is probably the Onyx 2000.

8 **Writing**

On a separate sheet of paper, write a paragraph about the city where you live. Use superlative forms to discuss the best and worst aspects of your city. Here are some topics you can write about:

- neighborhoods
- tourist sites
- parks
- restaurants
- hotels
- stores
- seasons

> I live in a small town called Roseland. The nicest area to live is on the north end. Unfortunately, that is also the most expensive area. The best restaurants and stores are in the center of town on Main Street. . . .

Chapters 18–19

A. Look at the chart. Complete the sentences below.

1. Derek Bridges is richer _____ most people.

2. Chris Wong is _____ than Elena Black.

3. Elena Black has _____ money than Chris Wong.

4. Elena Black earns the _____.

5. Derek Bridges has _____ money than me.

6. Chris Wong is not as rich _____ Derek Bridges.

7. Of these three people, Bridges earns the _____.

8. Bridges is the _____ of the three.

NAME	ANNUAL INCOME
Derek Bridges, millionaire	$1.6M
Chris Wong, doctor	$75,000
Elena Black, teacher	$25,000

B. Complete this speech with the words in the box. Some words can be used more than once.

as	better	does	fewer	least	less	more	most	than

Vote for me in the next election. I am _____ (9) interested in your needs than my opponent is. I have attended _____ (10) neighborhood meetings _____ (11) he has. That's because I feel more concern about our neighborhoods than he _____ (12).

My opponent isn't as concerned about local business _____ (13) I am. He has spoken to _____ (14) local businesspeople. Therefore, with business, too, he has shown _____ (15) interest than I have.

Of all past mayors, he has spent the _____ (16) money on schools, and he has spent the _____ (17) money on entertainment. He takes _____ (18) care of himself than your children's education! This is a disgrace! It's becoming more and _____ (19) obvious: I am a _____ (20) choice than my opponent. I will do the _____ (21) for our community.

C. Read the conversations in the chart. Check (✓) *OK* if the response is logical or *NOT OK* if the response is not logical.

	OK	NOT OK
22. **A:** I think the book is better than the movie. **B:** I agree. The movie is not as boring.		
23. **A:** These people have less money than we do. **B:** Yes. They're a lot wealthier.		
24. **A:** The weather is getting warmer and warmer. **B:** I think you're right. This winter is not as cold as winters in the past.		
25. **A:** That car gets a lot more miles per gallon than the old one. **B:** You're right. It's a lot less economical.		
26. **A:** This test was less difficult than the other tests. **B:** Yeah. It's the easiest test we've had.		
27. **A:** Why don't you do it? You have more time than me. **B:** That's not true! I'm just as busy as you are!		
28. **A:** I don't think that table is big enough for ten people. **B:** You're right. Let's look for a smaller one.		
29. **A:** There are fewer French classes than Spanish classes. **B:** Yes. At this school, French is less popular.		
30. **A:** Does Mexico City have the largest population of any city? **B:** Well, Mexico City has one of the largest populations. There are several other cities that are similar to it.		

Gerunds

FORM

Read this magazine article and complete the tasks below.

Exercise Your Way to Health!

Exercise is important for <u>staying</u> healthy. But what kind of exercise is best? The answer to this question depends on a person's physical condition 5 and his or her goals. For example, is the person simply trying to keep a basic level of fitness? Is losing weight the main goal?

The best exercises for maintaining 10 general health involve the whole body and increase a person's heart rate. Jogging, swimming, riding a bicycle, and playing tennis are good examples of such exercises. These kinds of exercises are 15 also very effective in helping a person to lose weight.

Increasing strength requires other kinds of exercises: A person needs to force a limited number of muscles 20 to do hard work within a short period of time. Gymnastics and weightlifting are examples of exercise that can help people improve strength. Doing both kinds of exercise—whole-body and concentrated 25 muscular work— helps a person achieve balance in his or her exercise routine and leads to the greatest health benefits.

People with health problems should talk with their doctor before they begin 30 exercising.

1. There are thirteen examples of words ending in –ing in the article. The first one is underlined. Underline twelve more.

2. One of these words is the present continuous form of a verb, rather than a gerund.

   Which word is it? _____

Working on Gerunds as Subjects

Complete these sentences with gerunds. Use the words and phrases in the box.

read/to children
skydive
not/eat/too many sweets
walk
watch/TV
join/a club

1. _Watching TV_____ is the most popular pastime in the United States.

2. _____ is a dangerous sport.

3. _____ is a good idea if you're on a diet.

4. _____ is a good way to meet people.

5. _____ helps them learn new words.

6. _____ is the cheapest form of exercise.

Working on Gerunds as Objects

Rewrite these sentences, using a gerund after the verb or verb phrase in parentheses. Make any other necessary changes.

1. It was great to work with you. (appreciated)

   _I appreciated working with you._____

2. It's OK with me if we leave early. (don't mind)

   _____

3. Min-hee hates to be late. (dislikes)

   _____

4. We might get a new car. (are considering)

   _____

5. Koji doesn't smoke anymore. (has quit)

   _____

6. He said to talk to you. (suggested)

   _____

4 Working on Gerunds after Prepositions

A. Complete these questions with the missing prepositions.

1. What is one thing you are looking forward _to_ right now?

   I'm looking forward to going away for the weekend.

2. When you are with your friends, what do you talk _____?

3. What do you sometimes worry _____?

4. What do you *not* approve _____?

5. What school subjects are you good _____?

6. What do you find it hard to get used _____?

7. What are you thinking _____ doing tonight?

8. What are you tired _____ right now?

9. What are you interested _____?

10. What are you planning _____ doing next summer?

B. Now write answers to the questions, using gerunds.

1. _____

2. _____

3. _____

4. _____

5. _____

6. _____

7. _____

8. _____

9. _____

10. _____

MEANING AND USE

Understanding Subject and Object Gerunds

A. Match the questions in Column 1 with the responses in Column 2.

Column 1

_f_ **1.** What do you usually do on Saturdays?

____ **2.** What sports do you like?

____ **3.** Why don't you wear a skirt?

____ **4.** I'm studying. Would you mind not talking so loudly?

____ **5.** How do you open this box?

____ **6.** Why can't we go in there?

____ **7.** Does your dad watch a lot of TV?

____ **8.** Would you mind giving us a ride home?

Column 2

a. Because I hate wearing skirts.

b. Because the sign says "No Trespassing."

c. No, of course not. I'm sorry.

d. I like swimming, windsurfing, and scuba diving.

e. Not at all. Where do you live?

f. I do my laundry, and then I go shopping.

g. Oh, yes. He loves watching old movies.

h. By turning it upside down. I'll help you.

B. Look again at the conversations. Find sentences in both columns that use gerunds in the following ways. Write them below.

1. to talk about liking or disliking activities

Because I hate wearing skirts.

_____

_____

2. to tell if an activity is permitted or not

_____

3. to talk about doing everyday activities

_____

4. to make a polite request

_____

_____

5. to talk about how something is done

_____

COMBINING FORM, MEANING, AND USE

 6 Editing

There are twelve errors in this e-mail message. The first one has been corrected. Find and correct eleven more.

To: Rosa Ramos
From: Donna Green
Cc:
Subject: Thank you!

Dear Rosa,

Thanks for ~~write~~ *writing* to me and especially for sending me the books. I really enjoyed to read them, especially *The Secret Diary of Elizabeth*. What a great story!

Anyway, I apologize for I didn't write back before now. I've been busy moving into my new apartment. It's more expensive than the old one, so I'm thinking about I might get a roommate. With a roommate, I can have more money to go ski, and I might even be able to save some money. Of course, the problem is finding someone I can live with. I've gotten used to live alone, and I'm not looking forward to share space with someone.

Also, I might look for another job. Writing letters are getting boring. And no getting along with my boss is unpleasant. I'm interested in move into a management position if I can find one. I wouldn't even mind to work part time for awhile.

So when are you coming to see my new apartment? You can stay here—if you don't mind to sleep on the sofa! Write back soon and let me know.

Love,

Donna

On a separate sheet of paper, write a letter to a friend. In your letter, do three of the following things. Use gerunds to:

- thank your friend for something.
- apologize for something.
- describe a plan for something.
- describe what you did last weekend.
- describe a new sport or hobby.
- invite your friend to do something.

Dear Ana,

    Thank you so much for inviting Donna and me to your house last weekend. We enjoyed staying with you and seeing your new place. . . .

21 Infinitives

FORM

1 Examining Form

Read this essay and complete the tasks below.

Happy Birthday!

A birthday is usually a happy occasion, so it's hard to imagine that in the past people considered birthdays to be dangerous. They believed that good and bad spirits followed a living person around. It was important to be very careful on a birthday because it was a time of change, and bad
5 spirits could do the most damage then.

Therefore, people had birthday parties in order to protect against bad spirits. At a party, friends and family come together to scare away the bad spirits. People gave presents and had a cake in order to help the good spirits and to bring good luck to the person having the birthday. If the person managed to blow out all the candles on
10 the cake, this helped to make his or her dreams come true.

It was common to put everyday objects such as coins, buttons, or rings inside the birthday cake. When the cake was cut, the person who found a particular object learned about his or her future. A coin meant wealth, and if someone found a ring, he or she could expect to marry soon.

1. Find three more examples of verb + (object +) infinitive and write them below.
   a. <u>considered birthdays to be</u>   c. _____
   b. _____   d. _____

2. Find four examples of (*in order*) + infinitive.
   a. _____   c. _____
   b. _____   d. _____

3. Find three examples of *it* (subject) . . . + infinitive.
   a. _____   c. _____
   b. _____

A. Rewrite these sentences, using infinitives.

1. He thinks he'll pass.

   He expects _to pass_____.

2. Please let me come too.

   I want _____.

3. We must get a new car.

   We need _____.

4. I'm not going to go to college.

   I've decided _____.

5. I won't tell anyone.

   I promise _____.

6. He wouldn't help us.

   He refused _____.

7. She said she can babysit the twins.

   She has agreed _____.

8. They said they would help us.

   They offered _____.

B. Choose the correct answer(s) to complete the sentences. More than one answer may be possible.

1. We need _____ the mail from the post office.

   (a.) you to pick up

   (b.) to pick up

2. It was cold, so Irina told _____ a jacket.

   a. to bring

   b. me to bring

3. I plan _____ tonight.

   a. us to go out

   b. to go out

4. Tony needs _____ the car to the garage.

   a. to take

   b. us to take

5. The police officer began _____ the accident.

   a. to describe

   b. them to describe

6. I expected _____ the race.

   a. our team to win

   b. to win

Completing Sentences with *It* Subject . . . + Infinitive

Use the words and phrases in the box to complete the sentences with *it* and an infinitive.

difficult/park the car	fun/watch movies at home
tiring/work all night	too expensive/buy a new one
not easy/find a job	important/exercise

1. I take the bus downtown every day because <u>it's difficult to park the car.</u>

2. I got a VCR because _____

3. Hector went back to school because _____

4. Our car is pretty old, but _____

5. Josh likes his night job even though _____

6. I don't exercise much, but I know that _____

MEANING AND USE

4 **Using Infinitives**

Use one item from each column and write six sentences with infinitives. Begin each sentence with *You use . . . .*

a saw	wash	your food
a broom	cut	clothes
a washing machine	hold	wood
a trash can	cook	the floor
a hose	water	the yard
a stove	sweep	trash

1. <u>You use a saw (in order) to cut wood.</u>

2. _____

3. _____

4. _____

5. _____

6. _____

5) Understanding Gerunds and Infinitives

Look at the chart. Complete the sentences with *going out, to going out, to go out.*
Check (✓) the correct column.

	(. . . *going out*)	(. . . *to going out*)	(. . . *to go out*)
1. <u>Do</u> you <u>enjoy</u>	✓		
2. I <u>don't mind</u>			
3. She's <u>looking forward</u>			
4. He <u>wanted</u>			
5. I'm <u>getting used</u>			
6. We <u>plan</u>			
7. She <u>expected</u>			
8. He <u>missed</u>			
9. I <u>disliked</u>			
10. We <u>are accustomed</u>			

6) Using Gerunds and Infinitives

Complete this story with the gerund or infinitive of the verbs in parentheses. In some
cases, both forms are correct.

I'm planning <u>to go</u> (go) to Europe this summer with my friends Julie and
                    1

Greg. I'm really looking forward to _____ (be) back in Paris again. Greg
                                        2

doesn't want _____ (spend) three weeks there, so Julie suggested
                3

_____ (meet) him there, and we've decided _____ (do) it that way.
    4   5

Julie really enjoys _____ (travel) to different countries. She wants
                        6

_____ (live) in Paris someday, but if she does, she'll have to get used to
    7

_____ (go) everywhere on public transportation. It's very difficult
    8

_____ (have) a car in Paris.
    9

I'm especially looking forward to _____ (not have) anything to do for
                                      10

three whole weeks. I expect _____ (spend) a lot of time at museums,
                               11

although I think Julie is planning _____ (go) shopping too. But she has
                                      12

promised _____ (not spend) so much money this year!
            13

Infinitives   125

COMBINING FORM, MEANING, AND USE

Choose the correct word or phrase to complete each conversation.

1. **Hiro:** Did you remember _____ that appointment?

   Satomi: Oh, no! I forgot. I'll do it right now.

   a. making

   (b.) to make

2. **Alex:** Tell us the whole story.

   Victor: Well, I remember _____ the restaurant, but I don't know what happened after that.

   a. leaving

   b. to leave

3. **Sara:** Dan, stop _____ the table.

   Dan: Sorry, Mom.

   a. kicking

   b. to kick

4. **Jake:** Dad, why are we slowing down?

   Paul: We're stopping _____ gas.

   a. getting

   b. to get

5. **Nesha:** Do you remember when the President was killed?

   Jada: Yes. I'll never forget _____ the words, "The President is dead."

   a. hearing

   b. to hear

6. **Min-woo:** What's that smell?

   Soo-jin: Oh, no! I forgot _____ off the stove!

   a. turning

   b. to turn

On a separate sheet of paper, write a paragraph about what happens in your country on one of these occasions:

- a birthday (of a child or an adult, or a special birthday)
- a visit to someone's home
- a holiday or festival

Use some infinitives. Here are some useful expressions and some verbs that are followed by infinitives.

EXPRESSIONS

It's the tradition/custom to . . . (or) It's customary to . . .

It's important (not) to . . .

VERBS

ask	tell	want
expect	plan	invite

    In my country, it's customary to bring a gift when someone invites you to their home for dinner. People don't expect you to bring a large or expensive gift, but it's important to show that you appreciate the invitation. . . .

22 Phrasal Verbs

FORM

1 **Examining Form**

Read these conversations at a party and complete the tasks below.

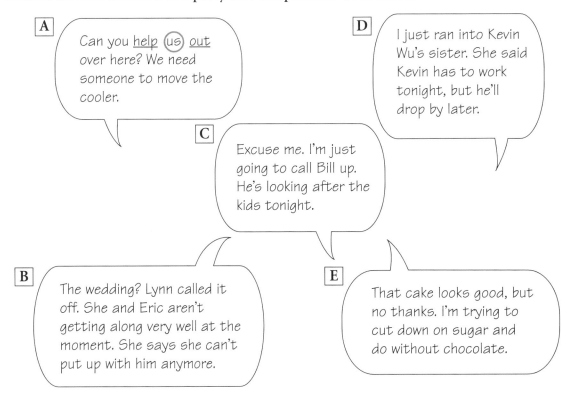

A Can you help (us) out over here? We need someone to move the cooler.

D I just ran into Kevin Wu's sister. She said Kevin has to work tonight, but he'll drop by later.

C Excuse me. I'm just going to call Bill up. He's looking after the kids tonight.

B The wedding? Lynn called it off. She and Eric aren't getting along very well at the moment. She says she can't put up with him anymore.

E That cake looks good, but no thanks. I'm trying to cut down on sugar and do without chocolate.

1. There are ten phrasal verbs in the conversations. The first one is underlined. Underline nine more.

2. Eight of the phrasal verbs have objects. The first one is circled. Find and circle seven more.

3. Complete this chart with the base forms of the underlined phrasal verbs.

   Transitive

   a. Inseparable: _look after_ _____ _____

   b. Three-word: _____ _____

   c. Separable: _____ _____ _____

   Intransitive: _____ _____

Working on Separable and Inseparable Phrasal Verbs

Use the words to write sentences.

1. out / leave / it

   Leave it out.

2. called / for / her / I

   _____

3. dropping off / it / she's

   _____

4. can't / do / it / I / without

   _____

5. it / over / reading / he's

   _____

6. after / looks / him / she

   _____

3 **Rewriting Sentences with Two-Word Verbs**

A. Complete the sentences below with the phrasal verbs in the box. Then put a *T* next to the sentences with transitive verbs and an *I* next to the sentences with intransitive verbs.

sit down	drop by	get along	turn down	put on	go over

   _T_ 1. Paulo has to _go over_ (his notes) tonight. He has a math test tomorrow.

   ____ 2. The Carsons are going to _____ on Sunday. It will be good to see them.

   ____ 3. Please _____ the music. It's too loud.

   ____ 4. Unfortunately, Ben and Kate don't _____. They fight all the time.

   ____ 5. It's going to snow today, so _____ your winter boots.

   ____ 6. Please come in and _____. Would you like some coffee?

B. Now circle the objects of the transitive verbs. Which two sentences can you change so that the object is between the verb and the particle? Write them that way.

   _____

   _____

   _____

MEANING AND USE

Choose the correct particle to complete each sentence.

1. I'm putting on weight again. I need to cut ____ on fat.

   a. in   **(b.)** down   **c.** off

2. I'm going to work late tonight. I have to go ____ my report before tomorrow.

   a. by   **b.** down   **c.** over

3. Be careful not to run ____ a lot of expenses.

   a. over   **b.** up   **c.** down

4. You have to get ____ of the car to see the view.

   a. down   **b.** in   **c.** out

5. I read your composition ____, and I liked it even better this time.

   a. down   **b.** over   **c.** out

6. Pedro really looks ____ to his father, and he wants to be a doctor just like him.

   a. over   **b.** by   **c.** up

Complete these sentences, replacing the one-word verbs with phrasal verbs. More than one phrasal verb may be possible.

1. They have canceled the game.

   They've _called off_____ the game.

2. I didn't find your gloves in the car.

   I didn't _____ your gloves in the car.

3. Please review your notes carefully.

   Please _____ your notes carefully.

4. You can omit this paragraph.

   You can _____ this paragraph.

5. I'll return the papers on Friday.

   I'll _____ the papers on Friday.

6. You must complete the form in our office.

   You must _____ the form in our office.

COMBINING FORM, MEANING, AND USE

Select verbs from the Phrasal Verbs chapter in the Student Book that you would like to be able to use correctly. Complete the information below for these verbs. For Type, say whether the phrasal verb is separable, inseparable, or intransitive.

1.

Phrasal verb	come across
Type	inseparable
Meaning	to find something
Chapter example	I came across your watch while I was cleaning.
My example	I came across some old vacation photos when I was packing my suitcase.

2.

Phrasal verb	
Type	
Meaning	
Chapter example	
My example	

3.

Phrasal verb	
Type	
Meaning	
Chapter example	
My example	

4.

Phrasal verb	
Type	
Meaning	
Chapter example	
My example	

On a separate sheet of paper, write a three-paragraph composition about your experience learning English and taking English classes.

1. In the first paragraph, write about positive experiences: good things about learning English, teachers that you have liked, and successes that you have had.

2. In the second paragraph, write about negative experiences—for example, disappointments and things that you find difficult.

3. In the third paragraph, write a short conclusion.

Use at least five phrasal verbs in your composition. Here are some verbs you can use (for others, see Appendix 17 in the Student Book).

figure out	look up	read over
help out	work out	do over
keep up	give back	go over
drop out	catch up with	put off
count on	fill out	put up with

When I first started to study English, I thought it would be hard to catch up with other people in class. However . . .

Later, English grammar and vocabulary became harder for me. I had to look up a lot of words and . . .

In conclusion, English can be easy in some ways and . . .

Chapters 20–22

A. Complete each sentence with the correct word or phrase.

1. _____ alone can be difficult at times.

   a. Living   **b.** Live

2. Avoid _____ your problems.

   a. thinking about   **b.** to think about

3. We're looking forward to _____ some time together.

   a. spending   **b.** spend

4. You can't learn a language just by _____ television.

   a. watching   **b.** watch

5. We're going to Denver _____ my grandparents.

   a. for visiting   **b.** to visit

6. I'll never get used to _____ famous.

   a. being   **b.** be

7. The workers expect _____ tomorrow.

   a. finishing   **b.** to finish

8. I didn't enjoy _____ the article.

   a. to read   **b.** reading

9. They told me _____ anything.

   a. not saying   **b.** not to say

10. Would you mind _____ the car for a minute?

    a. stopping   **b.** to stop

11. There's no point in _____ about that now.

    a. worrying   **b.** worry

12. We're thinking of _____ a house.

    a. buying   **b.** to buy

13. I'm sorry for _____ in touch, but we've been very busy.

    a. not being   **b.** not to be

14. The baby is starting _____ asleep.

    a. falling   **b.** to fall

15. I plan _____ my parents this weekend.

    a. visiting   **b.** to visit

B. Choose the correct word or phrase to complete each sentence.

16. **Gary:** Did you meet Janet?

    Malik: I don't remember _____ her.

    a. meeting   **b.** to meet

17. **Carlos:** Why isn't there any soda?

    Luisa: Because I stopped _____ soda.

    a. buying   **b.** to buy

18. **Rick:** Is Jeffrey still in bed?

    Sasha: Oh, no! I forgot _____ him up!

    a. waking   **b.** to wake

19. **Takeshi:** Tell the others I'll be late.

    Fumiko: Don't worry. I'll remember _____ them.

    a. telling   **b.** to tell

20. **Maria:** Are you still going out with Louise?

    Bob: No, I stopped _____ her.

    a. seeing   **b.** to see

21. **Lee:** That was a great vacation.

    Susan: Yes. I won't forget _____ the Grand Canyon.

    a. seeing   **b.** to see

C. Choose the correct word to complete each sentence. Use each word only once.

up	back	off	on	out	over	after	with	into

22. My brother dropped _____ of high school and started his own business.

23. My teacher is planning to give _____ our papers.

24. It's getting dark. Please turn _____ the lights.

25. I'll pick _____ some milk on my way home.

26. When the parents died, there was nobody to look _____ the children.

27. We'll have to call _____ the picnic if it rains.

28. My husband doesn't get along _____ his boss very well.

29. I ran _____ an old school friend this morning.

30. I'll feel more comfortable if I go _____ my speech again.

Answer Key

Chapter 1 The Simple Present

Exercise 1 (p. 1)

1. line 3:   helps
   line 4:   doesn't complain
   line 5:   remembers
   line 6:   is
   line 7:   loves
   line 7:   love
   line 8:   have
   line 9:   doesn't talk
   line 10: goes
   line 11: comes
   line 12: watches
   line 12: talks
   line 14: sits
   line 15: don't know
   line 15: isn't
   line 16: doesn't seem
   line 18: don't go
   line 19: don't have
   line 20: need
   line 21: doesn't understand
   line 22: do...have

2. simple present

Exercise 2 (p. 2)

2. enjoy
3. see
4. talks
5. argue
6. don't talk
7. watch
8. fixes
9. eats
10. don't get

Exercise 3 (p. 2)

But she speaks English at work and with some friends. Sometimes her friends correct her pronunciation. She doesn't mind that; she thinks it helps her.

Her listening skills are pretty good. She listens to songs in English. She watches movies in English, too. Her brother watches them with her.

Reading and writing are more difficult for her. She doesn't read English very often, and she almost never writes it. She thinks her writing has a lot of grammar mistakes, but maybe she worries too much.

Exercise 4 (p. 3)

A. 2. Are
   3. Do
   4. Are
   5. Does
   6. Is
   7. Is
   8. Does

B. b. 7   c. 2   d. 5   e. 6   f. 8   g. 1   h. 3

Exercise 5 (p. 4)

2. do most people go to work?
3. people use public transportation to go to work?
4. do most people retire?
5. televisions do most families have?
6. do many people do after high school?
7. do most Americans move?
8. do most American women marry?

Exercise 6 (p. 5)

A. 2. f
   3. a
   4. b
   5. c
   6. e

B. b. 1   c. 5   d. 2   e. 4   f. 3

Exercise 7 (p. 6)

The two seasons ~~is~~ *are* summer and winter. Summer ~~go~~ *goes* from April to October. In summer it gets very hot. The temperature sometimes ~~reach~~ *reaches* 40° Celsius. It also ~~rain~~ *rains* a lot in summer. Winter in my country ~~Begin~~ *begins* in November. In winter, it is cooler, and it ~~not~~ *does* rain very much. I like the weather better in the winter because I ~~no~~ *don't* like hot weather.

Exercise 8 (p. 6)

Answers will vary.

Chapter 2 Imperatives

Exercise 1 (p. 7)
1. line 4: Go   line 9:   Drive
   line 5: Turn   line 10: Turn
   line 7: Stay   line 14: Drive
   line 8: Make   line 15: call
2. Yes, but we don't usually say or write the subject *(you)* when using imperatives.

Exercise 2 (p. 8)
2. Let go of the hand brake.
3. Put the car into drive.
4. Check the rearview mirror.
5. Turn the steering wheel to the right.
6. Don't go so fast.

Exercise 3 (p. 8)
2. have
3. Know
4. don't panic
5. don't go
6. go
7. check
8. don't move
9. don't use

Exercise 4 (p. 9)
2. a
3. h
4. c
5. d
6. b
7. f
8. g

Exercise 5 (p. 9)
2. Check   7. Fasten
3. Arrive   8. drink
4. Bring   9. Chew
5. Remove   10. Enjoy
6. listen

Exercise 6 (p. 10)
2. Let me see, please.   request
3. Don't worry about it.   advice
4. Have a seat.   offer
5. Get up!   command
6. Look out!   warning

Exercise 7 (p. 11)
Answers will vary.

Exercise 8 (p. 11)
Answers will vary.

Chapter 3 The Present Continuous

Exercise 1 (p. 12)
1. line 5: is breaking   line 6:   's blowing
   line 6: 's waiting   line 11: 'm leaving
2. *be* + base form of verb + *ing*

Exercise 2 (p. 13)
2. 'm looking
3. is shining
4. are playing
5. 're wearing
6. 're not thinking/aren't thinking
7. 're having
8. is spraying
9. 're not/aren't running
10. 're trying
11. 's not/isn't letting
12. is telling
13. 's not/isn't paying
14. are laughing
15. 're getting

Exercise 3 (p. 14)
2. How are your friends traveling?
3. Who's the boss talking to?
4. Why is that child crying?
5. Where are Susan and John going?
6. Who's following us?

Exercise 4 (p. 14)
2. It's raining
3. It rains
4. it's raining
5. It rains
6. it's raining
7. It rains
8. It's raining

Exercise 5 (p. 15)
1. b. He's studying in the library at the moment.
   c. My favorite TV show is starting.
2. a. I'm taking three science classes this semester.
   b. For now, I'm staying with Maria.
   c. Luisa and I are trying to get an apartment together.
3. And rents are going up all the time.
4. a. I don't have an apartment right now.
   b. But the apartments seem very expensive.

Exercise 6 (p. 16)

2. 're talking, don't understand
3. 're building, doesn't have
4. doesn't seem, 's working
5. thinks, 's not/isn't studying
6. Do (you) know, 's acting

Exercise 7 (p. 16)

Answers will vary.

See page 151 for Key to Review: Chapters 1–3.

Chapter 4 The Simple Past

Exercise 1 (p. 19)

1. line 2: were   line 7: was
   line 3: was   line 16: was
   line 4: was   line 21: wasn't

2. line 8: tried   line 18: returned
   line 10: believed line 20: wanted
   line 15: loved   line 22: advised

3. line 12: went   line 15: found
   line 14: took   line 20: told

Exercise 2 (p. 20)

2. were
3. was
4. were
5. was
6. was
7. were
8. were

Exercise 3 (p. 20)

I learned a lot in his class. First, he explained things clearly. When two words had similar meanings, he showed us the difference in a simple way. Time went by quickly in his class. We didn't get bored.

Mr. Kennedy didn't have favorites. He spent time with everyone. He didn't make comments about the weaker students. He encouraged them and helped them a lot. He knew everyone's name by the second class. He was everyone's favorite teacher, and he really enjoyed teaching.

Exercise 4 (p. 21)

2. Were your parents very happy in Colombia?
3. Did your parents come to the U.S. in 1998?
4. Did your father want to move to the U.S.?
5. Were your sisters homesick at first?
6. Did your father find work?

Exercise 5 (p. 21)

2. a. What did Leonardo da Vinci paint?
   b. Who painted the *Mona Lisa*?
3. a. What began in 1848?
   b. When did the California Gold Rush begin?
4. a. Who won the Nobel Peace Prize in 1993?
   b. When did Nelson Mandela win the Nobel Peace Prize?

Exercise 6 (p. 22)

1. b, c
2. d, e
3. a, b
4. c, d, e

Exercise 7 (p. 22)

2. I used to go there every summer.
3. No change
4. I used to love working on the farm.
5. I used to take very good care of the animals.
6. No change

Exercise 8 (p. 23)

I was sad when I left my home country, especially
            said
when I ~~say~~ good-bye to my friends.
                                        wasn't
    At the beginning, living in the U.S. ~~isn't~~ easy for me.
                              was
In those days, the language ~~is~~ hard for me because I
didn't   *didn't*
~~don't~~ speak it very well. Also, my parents ~~don't~~ speak
                              helped
English at all then, so I ~~help~~ them. A few months after I
                                        became
came here, I met some people who ~~become~~ my friends.
         made
This ~~makes~~ a big difference in my life at that time. After I
met   *felt*
~~meet~~ them, I ~~feel~~ more confident.
                              have
    Now I am going to school, I ~~had~~ some friends, and my

English is better, too.

Exercise 9 (p. 23)

Answers will vary.

Chapter 5 The Past Continuous and Past Time Clauses

Exercise 1 (p. 24)

line 3:   were flashing
line 9:   was crying
line 10: were holding
line 11: was going down

line 13: was raining
line 16: were rushing
line 21: were waiting

Exercise 2 (p. 25)

2. We were eating lunch in the cafeteria
3. You were sitting on the deck
4. The sun was shining
5. The boys were walking to the park

Exercise 3 (p. 25)

2. Who were you studying with?
3. Where were you studying?
4. Why were you studying?
5. Where were you sitting?

Exercise 4 (p. 26)

2. After the rain stopped, we walked home.
3. When Keiko got home, she was exhausted.
4. Hanna moved to Los Angeles after she graduated from college.
5.   While Paulo was on his vacation, he felt relaxed.

Exercise 5 (p. 26)

2. a
3. b
4. b
5. a

Exercise 6 (p. 27)

2. b   7. b
3. b   8. a
4. b   9. b
5. a   10. a
6. a

Exercise 7 (p. 28)

A.   2. T
         3. T
         4. F
         5. F
         6. T
         7. F
         8. T
         9. T
        10. F

B.   4. He made copies after he took notes in the meeting.
         5. He made copies after he took notes in the meeting.
         7. While Bob was making phone calls, the fax machine jammed.
        10. Bob went to lunch after he received a fax.

Exercise 8 (p. 29)

When I was reaching [*reached*] to the corner of Broadway and Stockton, I stopped because the light was red. I was waiting for the light to change, and suddenly someone was tapping [*tapped*] me once on the shoulder. Who was it? I turned around to find out. A man were [*was*] standing behind me. When the light changed, I began to walk really fast. But every time I looked behind me, I was seeing [*saw*] the man. Finally, I went into a drugstore to escape him. Ten minutes later I was coming [*came*] out. The man was still outside! He came up to me and spoke. "Are you Susie Lin?" he asked. "I'm your cousin from Vancouver."

Exercise 9 (p. 29)

Answers will vary.

Chapter 6 The Present Perfect

Exercise 1 (p. 30)

1. line 15: have visited   line 19: have been
   line 16: have...traveled   line 27: has covered

2. *have/has* + past participle

Exercise 2 (p. 31)

2. ridden
3. eaten
4. met
5. flown
6. found

Answers: Yes, I have/No, I haven't.

Exercise 3 (p. 31)

2. Where have you traveled to?
3. How many people has she invited?
4. Who has been to China?
5. Why have you chosen that book?
6. How long has Larry lived there?
7. What have you prepared for lunch?
8. How much money have you spent this week?

Exercise 4 (p. 32)

2. b
3. a
4. b
5. b
6. a

Exercise 5 (p. 32)

2. since
3. for
4. for
5. since
6. for
7. since
8. since

Exercise 6 (p. 33)

2. 've wanted/have wanted
3. left
4. worked
5. was
6. played
7. gave
8. worked
9. 've had/have had
10. Have you ever had
11. 've looked after/have looked after

Exercise 7 (p. 33)

Answers will vary. Some examples are:

2. We've raised $5,700 so far. / So far we've raised $5,700. / We've already raised $5,700. / We've raised $5,700 already.
3. He's never been to Europe. / He hasn't been to Europe yet. / He still hasn't been to Europe. / He hasn't been to Europe so far. / So far he hasn't been to Europe.
4. They've already interviewed five people. / They've interviewed five people already. / They've interviewed five people so far. / So far they've interviewed five people.

Exercise 8 (p. 34)

We've visited cousins in Australia, and we ^'ve been to New Zealand twice. We've also ~~went~~ gone on safari in Africa. We've been to Europe a lot. Gina and I ~~has~~ have spent time in Paris, in Madrid, and in several cities in Italy. We haven't ^been/gone to Eastern Europe yet, though. We hope to visit Prague and Budapest next year.

My sister Betty was born in the United States, and she has never traveled outside the country—except once when she was very young. But she ~~have~~ has been to a lot of places in the U.S. She has ~~visit~~ visited most of the national parks: the Grand Canyon, Yellowstone, Yosemite, and so on. She has been to all of the big cities, too. In fact, she ~~is~~ has lived in four different cities in the U.S.: New York, Boston, Los Angeles, and San Francisco. I think she ^'s seen more of her own country than most people.

Exercise 9 (p. 34)

Answers will vary.

See page 151 for Key to Review: Chapters 4–6.

Chapter 7 Future Time: *Be Going To, Will, and the Present Continuous*

Exercise 1 (p. 37)

1. line 13: 'm going to clean
   line 15: is going to give
   line 16: 's going to help
2. line 11: won't need   line 13: will be
   line 11: 'll save   line 16: 'll be
   line 12: 'll . . . save   line 17: 'll write
3. line 6: 're moving in

Exercise 2 (p. 38)

2. Are you going to have a big wedding?
3. We're not/We aren't going to have a big celebration.
4. Is it going to rain tomorrow?
5. What are you going to do?
6. I'm going to stay home and read a book.

Exercise 3 (p. 38)

2. When will he find out the results?
3. Where will we/you go?
4. Who will be there?
5. When/What time will the photos be ready?
6. How long will it take?

Exercise 4 (p. 39)

He'll get back at 6:45, take a shower, and shave. He'll go downstairs at 7:00. He'll make a cup of coffee, but he won't drink it. He'll take it with him in his car. He won't eat anything, either. Then he'll drive to work. He'll have breakfast at his desk.

Exercise 5 (p. 39)

A. 2. e
   3. f
   4. c
   5. a
   6. b

B. a. 5   b. 2, 6   c. 3, 4

Exercise 6 (p. 40)

1. b. I think we're going to hike up the mountain.
2. a. They say the weather's going to be bad.
   b. You're going to get very wet.
3. a. When are you leaving?
   b. We're leaving here on Wednesday.
   c. Then we're flying home on Sunday.
   d. Where are you going in between?
   e. What are you doing tomorrow?
4. a. Are you and Kate having a good vacation here in Colorado?
   b. We're having a wonderful time.

Exercise 7 (p. 41)

2. S
3. D
4. S
5. S
6. D

Exercise 8 (p. 41)

2. b
3. a
4. a
5. b
6. b

Exercise 9 (p. 42)

Answers will vary.

Chapter 8 Future Time Clauses and *If* Clauses

Exercise 1 (p. 43)

1. line 16: she will be a good student
   line 18: he will travel far
   line 20: she will love food
   line 21: he will become a musician
   The tense used in the main clauses is future with *will*.
2. simple present

Exercise 2 (p. 44)

2. We'll eat / We're going to eat dinner
3. I'll cash / I'm going to cash my paycheck
4. when he turns 68
5. I won't be / I'm not going to be upset
6. we'll celebrate / we're going to celebrate
7. I'll buy / I'm going to buy a new car
8. If you drive too fast

Exercise 3 (p. 44)

2. I'll be ready to leave after I say good-bye to the children.
3. If we don't invite Eric to the party, Sun-Hee will be angry.
4. When Victor gets here, we're going to pick up the car.
5. I'm not going to go swimming if the water's too cold.
6. When the guests arrive, dinner will be ready.

7. If they have another baby, they'll buy a bigger house.
8. I'll look for a job in San Francisco after I graduate.

Exercise 4 (p. 45)

Answers will vary.

Exercise 5 (p. 45)

1. h
2. a, d
3. b, f
4. c, g

Exercise 6 (p. 46)

2. b
3. a
4. b

Exercise 7 (p. 46)

2. If Reiko does well in the interview, she'll get the job. / Reiko will get the job if she does well in the interview.
3. After I lose 10 pounds, I'm going to join a gym. / I'm going to join a gym after I lose 10 pounds.
4. When the movie ends, I'll call you. / I'll call you when the movie ends.
5. If we make too much noise, the baby will wake up. / The baby will wake up if we make too much noise.
6. We're going to eat dinner before we listen to the radio. / Before we listen to the radio, we're going to eat dinner.
7. After Matt buys the groceries, he will go to the bank. / Matt will go to the bank after he buys the groceries.
8. If Ana reads more books, she will increase her vocabulary. / Ana will increase her vocabulary if she reads more books.

Exercise 8 (p. 47)

Answers will vary.

See page 151 for Key to Review: Chapters 7–8.

Chapter 9 Modals of Ability and Possibility

Exercise 1 (p. 50)

1. line 4: can   line 8: Can
   line 4: will   line 8: might not
   line 6: will   line 9: can
   line 6: may   line 9: could
   line 7: won't

2. ✓ Each modal has only one form.
                    don't
   _____ Modals ∧agree with the subject.

Exercise 2 (p. 51)

A. 2. I can't ski.
   3. Can you drive?
   4. They can play several instruments.

B. 1. We couldn't see anything.
   2. Could you play the piano when you were younger?
   3. They couldn't tell me anything.
   4. Could Tomek understand that?

Exercise 3 (p. 51)

A. 2. When could he get here?
   3. How long could it take?
   4. What could go wrong?

B. 1. What kind of car will you get?
   2. How will you pay the bills?
   3. What time will he get there?
   4. Who will be there?

Exercise 4 (p. 52)

2. can't, will be able to
3. can, will be able to
4. won't be able to
5. won't be able to, will be able to
6. will be able to

Exercise 5 (p. 53)

2. Correct
3. Incorrect, was able to
4. Correct
5. Incorrect, were able to

Exercise 6 (p. 53)

LESS CERTAINTY	MORE CERTAINTY
2.	eat dinner
3. study English	
4. read a book	
5. watch TV	
6.	go to bed before midnight

Exercise 7 (p. 54)

2. b
3. b
4. c
5. a
6. b

Exercise 8 (p. 54)

Answers will vary.

Chapter 10 Modals and Phrases of Request, Permission, Desire, and Preference

Exercise 1 (p. 55)

2. C, Could
3. B, Can
4. A, would
5. C, Would

6. A, 'd
7. B, Can
8. A, 'd
9. B, Could
10. C, 'd

Exercise 2 (p. 56)

2. May I have some more coffee?
3. Would you take my picture?
4. When could I see you tomorrow?
5. Can I have something to eat?
6. Will you give me a ride?

Exercise 3 (p. 56)

2. I'd prefer not to take a class on Fridays.
3. What time would Takeshi like to leave?
4. My mother would rather not come with us.
5. Would you prefer milk or juice?
6. I'd like to live in a big city.

Exercise 4 (p. 57)

2. a. Can I talk to you after class?
   b. May I please talk to you after class?
3. a. Can you say that again?
   b. Would you say that again, please?
4. a. Would you drop me off at the corner, please?
   b. Can you drop me off at the corner?

Exercise 5 (p. 57)

2. 'd prefer
3. 'd rather
4. 'd rather
5. Would...like
6. 'd like
7. Would...prefer/Would...like
8. 'd like

Exercise 6 (p. 58)

2. b
3. a
4. a
5. c
6. b
7. b
8. c
9. b
10. a

Exercise 7 (p. 59)

Answers will vary.

Chapter 11 Modals and Phrasal Modals of Advice, Necessity, and Prohibition

Exercise 1 (p. 60)

1. line 6:   could
    line 11: must
    line 12: should
    line 15: 'd better

    line 19: should
    line 24: ought to
    line 29: have to
    line 33: should

2. line 6:   collect
    line 11: consider
    line 12: try
    line 15: choose

    line 19: learn
    line 24: know
    line 29: know
    line 33: be

Exercise 2 (p. 61)

2. to go
3. to go
4. go
5. go
6. go
7. to go
8. to go
9. go
10. to go

Exercise 3 (p. 61)

2. Who should she tell?
3. When do they have to leave?
4. How long do you have to stay?
5. When does he have to tell her?
6. What should Emily do?
7. Who should I ask?
8. How often should we exercise?

Exercise 4 (p. 62)

2. b
3. b
4. a
5. b
6. b

Exercise 5 (p. 62)

Chris: You ~~could~~ *must/have (got) to* show your passport and your visa.

Satomi: OK. And how do I get to the university?

Chris: Well, you ~~have~~ *could/might* to take public transportation, but it's probably better to take a taxi.

Satomi: How much will that cost?

Chris: About $30. But you ~~might~~ *should/ought* add a tip for the taxi driver. That's my advice—almost everyone tips. We usually tip about 15 percent.

Satomi: I see. What about money? What's the best way to keep my money?

Chris: Well, you could use traveler's checks, or you ~~must~~ *could/might* open a bank account.

Exercise 6 (p. 63)

2. must
3. must not
4. must
5. must
6. don't have to
7. must
8. must
9. don't have to

Exercise 7 (p. 63)

2. a
3. b
4. b
5. a
6. a

Exercise 8 (p. 64)

Answers will vary.

See page 152 for Key to Review: Chapters 9–11.

Chapter 12 Tag Questions

Exercise 1 (p. 67)

1. 2. c
    3. f
    4. a
    5. e
    6. d
2. b. "It's beautiful, <u>isn't it?</u>"
    c. "You *do* know the way, <u>don't you?</u>"
    d. "She looks just like her father, <u>doesn't she?</u>"
    e. "It's warm in here, <u>isn't it?</u>"
    f. "You couldn't help me with this, <u>could you?</u>"
3. affirmative statements
4. negative statements

Exercise 2 (p. 68)

2. doesn't she
3. will it
4. aren't I
5. do you
6. hasn't he
7. isn't it
8. can he

Exercise 3 (p. 68)

2. Yes, I do
3. Yes, we are
4. No, I haven't
5. Yes, they did
6. Yes, I will
7. No, they don't
8. Yes, you are

Exercise 4 (p. 69)

2. a
3. b
4. a

Exercise 5 (p. 69)

2. You don't have an extra pen, do you?
3. You couldn't wait until tomorrow, could you?
4. You wouldn't be able to work late today, would you?
5. You couldn't come here a little earlier, could you?
6. You don't know what time it is, do you?

Exercise 6 (p. 70)

2. Conversation 2, 4
3. Conversation 1

Exercise 7 (p. 70)

We've never met before, have we?
Lauren looks beautiful, doesn't she?
And you're a friend of Tony's, aren't you?
You and he work at Intellek, don't you?
That's Lauren's father, isn't it?

Exercise 8 (p. 71)

Answers will vary.

Chapter 13 Additions with Conjunctions

Exercise 1 (p. 72)

1. line 9:   Mark is tall and fair, and so is Matt.
   line 12: But Lisa couldn't do math, and neither could Julie.
   line 13: In fact, Lisa failed math in ninth grade, and Julie did, too.
   line 17: Lisa had a boy and then a girl, and so did Julie.
   line 26: Lisa can't explain any of this, and Julie can't either.
2. affirmative sentences

Exercise 2 (p. 73)

2. and, either
3. and, too
4. and, too
5. but
6. and, either
7. but
8. and, either
9. but
10. and, too

Exercise 3 (p. 73)

2. so
3. either
4. do
5. did
6. neither

7. have
8. doesn't
9. too
10. can't
11. doesn't
12. isn't

Exercise 4 (p. 74)

2. So did I.
3. Neither do I.
4. Neither did I.
5. So do I.
6. Neither can I.

Exercise 5 (p. 74)

2. Cats are popular pets, and so are dogs.
3. Kangaroos are not native to the U.S., and koalas aren't either.
4. Kangaroos come from Australia, and koalas do too.
5. Tigers don't live in groups, and neither do leopards.
6. Lions have killed people, and so have tigers.

Exercise 6 (p. 75)

Answers will vary. Some examples are:
2. Ben doesn't have brothers and sisters, but Kevin and Chris do.
3. Chris has been to Disneyland, and Ben has too.
4. Chris didn't go to preschool, and neither did Ben.
5. Ben can read a little, and so can Kevin.
6. Ben and Kevin can swim, but Chris can't.
7. Kevin doesn't like spinach, and Chris doesn't like it either.
8. Kevin would like a bike for his birthday, and so would Ben.

Exercise 7 (p. 76)

Answers will vary.

See page 152 for Key to Review: Chapters 12–13.

Chapter 14 Nouns and Quantity Expressions

Exercise 1 (p. 79)

1. line 4:   a few   line 19: much
   line 10: many   line 20: many
   line 11: several   line 22: much
   line 12: a great deal of line 25: no
   line 17: any   line 28: some
   line 18: a lot of

2. *Count nouns*
   line 5:   dollars   line 18: hours
   line 10: expenses   line 20: things
   line 11: cars   line 25: job
   line 17: problems

Noncount nouns
line 12: money
line 19: time
line 22: information
line 28: work

Exercise 2 (p. 80)

2. b
3. a
4. a
5. b
6. a
7. b
8. a

Exercise 3 (p. 80)

2. cup
3. can
4. slice
5. drop
6. bunch
7. carton
8. jar
9. bag
10. pile

Exercise 4 (p. 81)

A. 2. A lot of
3. Quite a few
4. Some
5. Very few
6. no

B. 1. a great deal of
2. quite a lot of
3. some
4. very little

Exercise 5 (p. 82)

A. 2. Here are some assignments for you.
3. There are a lot of assignments for this class.
4. She gives very few assignments.
5. We don't have any assignments tonight.
6. Please don't give us so many assignments.

B. 1. I have a little work for you.
2. There is no work in this town.
3. How much work is available?
4. There isn't much interesting work.
5. This is essential work.
6. There is very little work here.

Exercise 6 (p. 83)

A. 2. How much
3. How much
4. How many
5. How much
6. How much
7. How many
8. How many

B. 1. Answers will vary.

Exercise 7 (p. 83)

Answers will vary.

Chapter 15 Indefinite and Definite Articles

Exercise 1 (p. 84)

1. **Indefinite articles**

line 2:	an	line 9:	a
line 5:	a	line 10:	an
line 6:	an	line 11:	an
line 8:	a	line 15:	a

Definite articles

line 7:	the	line 13:	The
line 8:	the	line 13:	the
line 9:	The	line 14:	the
line 9:	the	line 14:	the
line 10:	the	line 14:	the
line 11:	the	line 15:	the
line 12:	The		

Answers for *2a, 2b,* and *2e* can be any two of the answers below.

2. **a.** an American artist, a young woman, an open field, a group, a farm, an angle, an interesting painting, a place
b. the painting, the sun, The woman, the viewer, the idea, the world
c. the hopefulness, the courage
d. The buildings, the things
e. loneliness, sadness, hope

Exercise 2 (p. 85)

2. a
3. an
4. a
5. an
6. a
7. an
8. an
9. an
10. a

Exercise 3 (p. 85)

Conversation 1: 2. a   3. the   4. a
Conversation 2: 1. the   2. a   3. the   4. the
Conversation 3: 1. a   2. The   3. an   4. a
                  5. a   6. the

Exercise 4 (p. 86)

1. 2
2. 4
3. 3
4. 6
5. 5

Exercise 5 (p. 86)

2. a/the
3. a
4. the
5. the
6. a
7. a
8. a
9. the
10. the
11. the
12. the

Exercise 6 (p. 87)

A. Answers will vary.

B. 1. Time, (Bad) news, Love
2. Beggars, Children
3. A leopard, A friend
4. The (early) bird, The pen

Exercise 7 (p. 88)

. . . in ~~the~~ business and in everyday life. In my life as ^a∧

student, computers help me in a couple of ways.

First, computers help me communicate with people.

Every day I check my e-mail. I often have ~~the~~ messages

from my family or from a friend. E-mail saves me a lot

of ~~the~~ time and money. I don't have to wait for letters

or stand in line at ^{the/a}∧ post office to buy ~~the~~ stamps. At

^{the}∧ university where I study, students can communicate with

their teachers by e-mail. I sometimes use e-mail to send

^{an}∧ assignment.

Second, my computer helps me prepare my

assignments. If I have ~~the~~^a paper to write, I can search the

Internet to get ~~an~~ information. The word-processing

program on ^{the}∧ computer makes it easy to write many drafts.

The program checks grammar and spelling. When I make

~~the~~ mistakes, the program marks them so I can find and

correct them.

Exercise 8 (p. 88)

Answers will vary.

See page 152 for Key to Review: Chapters 14–15.

Chapter 16 Adjectives

Exercise 1 (p. 91)

1.   2. famous
3. special
4. elegant black wool
5. unusual
6. relaxing
7. excellent
8. creamed red
9. fresh local
10. previous
11. happy
12. new
13. ancient Indian
14. beautiful
15. pink silk sleeveless
16. white straw

Exercise 2 (p. 92)

A. 2. painful
3. stressful
4. successful

B. 1. pointless
2. careless
3. homeless
4. hopeless

C. 1. comfortable
2. knowledgeable
3. valuable
4. profitable

D. 1. shady
2. rusty
3. salty
4. dirty

E. 1. heroic
2. poetic
3. diplomatic
4. athletic

Exercise 3 (p. 93)

2. The actor was tall, dark, and handsome.
3. My previous boss is a rich man.
4. I didn't buy anything special.
5. This tree is over thirty years old.
6. We had a difficult, tiring trip. / We had a tiring, difficult trip.

Exercise 4 (p. 93)

2. They have a beautiful wooden dining room table.
3. Enjoy a glass of delicious mineral water.
4. I'm going to wear my comfortable old running shoes.
5. I love my old black typewriter.
6. He has an expensive new car.

Exercise 5 (p. 94)

2. terrified
3. annoyed
4. boring
5. embarrassing
6. tiring
7. amazed
8. excited

Exercise 6 (p. 95)

Answers will vary. Some examples are:

2. short
3. black
4. leather
5. long
6. striped
7. tight
8. fashionable
9. high
10. odd

Exercise 7 (p. 95)

Answers will vary.

Chapter 17 Adverbs

Exercise 1 (p. 96)

b. slowly
c. sadly
d. carefully, desperately, quietly

Exercise 2 (p. 97)

2. adverb
3. adverb
4. adjective
5. adverb
6. adverb
7. adjective
8. adjective
9. adverb
10. adverb

Exercise 3 (p. 97)

2. I admire Jake tremendously.
3. The President appeared briefly.
4. Chris and Gina argue constantly.
5. Marta writes very well.
6. She hugged the children lovingly.

Exercise 4 (p. 98)

2. The hurricane hit the Florida coast hard.
3. We're probably going to move.
4. It's definitely not raining hard.
5. You obviously didn't like him. / Obviously, you didn't like him. / You didn't like him, obviously.
6. Maybe she speaks Spanish well.
7. Yesterday he drove carefully. / He drove carefully yesterday.
8. She certainly dances beautifully.

Exercise 5 (p. 98)

Answers will vary. Some examples are:

2. such a good
3. so near/close
4. such bad/wet/terrible
5. such big/large
6. such a warm
7. such good
8. so fast

Exercise 6 (p. 99)

1. b. quietly, works
   c. hard, (is) working
   d. smoothly, are moving
   e. dramatically, have risen
   f. confidently, move
2. today, recently, now, soon
3. obviously
4. certainly, probably

Exercise 7 (p. 100)

2. That suitcase isn't big enough to hold all my clothes.
   That suitcase is too small to hold all my clothes.
3. I get home too late to watch that show.
   I don't get home early enough to watch that show.
4. That computer is too slow to handle the job.
   That computer isn't fast enough to handle the job.

Exercise 8 (p. 100)

2. b
3. a
4. b
5. a
6. b

Exercise 9 (p. 101)

Answers will vary.

Exercise 10 (p. 101)

Answers will vary.

See page 153 for Key to Review: Chapters 16–17.

Chapter 18 Comparatives

Exercise 1 (p. 104)

1. line 4:   higher
   line 4:   more expensive
   line 5:   larger
   line 6:   better
   line 9:   richer
   line 10: happier
   line 23: more beautiful
   line 24: newer
   line 34: more relaxed
   line 40: younger

2. line 21: better
   line 28: harder
   line 33: more fully

3. line 3:   more money
   line 35: more time
   line 39: more problems

Exercise 2 (p. 105)

2. bigger
3. more quickly
4. closer
5. happier
6. more softly
7. thinner
8. healthier
9. better
10. more satisfied
11. more comfortable
12. worse

Exercise 3 (p. 105)

2. more attractive
3. more conveniently
4. closer
5. later
6. sunnier
7. bigger
8. smaller
9. more spacious
10. better
11. more efficiently
12. cheaper

Exercise 4 (p. 106)

2. am
3. her/she
4. does/works
5. did/got
6. can
7. is
8. me/I

Exercise 5 (p. 106)

Answers may vary. Some examples are:
2. My brother isn't as old as I am.
3. You speak as fluently as she (does/speaks).
4. Amy takes as many classes as he (does/takes).
5. They aren't as friendly as she is.
6. Kevin works as hard as they (do/work).
7. They travel as much as we do.
8. Luisa watches as much TV as I do.

Exercise 6 (p. 107)

2. more money than we (do/have)/than us
3. more foreign language students than
4. less work than Stefan (does)
5. more information than the other one (does/has)
6. fewer TVs than the Smiths (do/own)

Exercise 7 (p. 107)

2. Biology is easier than physics (is).
3. Larry doesn't write as well as me/I (do/write).
4. Adults are more polite than children (are).
5. My dog doesn't bark as loudly as the neighbor's dog (does/barks).
6. Evening traffic is worse than morning traffic (is).

Exercise 8 (p. 108)

Answers will vary. Some examples are:
2. A coat is thicker and warmer (than a raincoat). A raincoat is not as warm (as a coat), but it is more waterproof.
3. A hardcover book is heavier and more expensive; it isn't as easy to carry as a paperback. A paperback is thinner, lighter, and cheaper.
4. An airplane is faster and flies higher (than a helicopter). A helicopter is not as fast (as an airplane), and it flies lower.

Exercise 9 (p. 108)

Answers will vary.

Chapter 19 Superlatives

Exercise 1 (p. 109)

1. line 6:   the driest   line 19: the most destructive
   line 7:   the wettest   line 28: the heaviest
   line 18: the most   line 33: the hottest
             powerful

2. *the* + adjective + *-est*
   (Make spelling changes as necessary.)

3. *the most* + adjective

Exercise 2 (p. 110)

2. the hardest
3. the most unusual
4. the most expensive
5. the longest
6. the fastest
7. the most efficient
8. the worst

Exercise 3 (p. 110)

2. He works the hardest.
3. He's the most reliable.
4. He arrives the earliest.
5. He does the most work.
6. He's the most popular with the customers.
7. He works the most carefully.
8. He is the friendliest.

Exercise 4 (p. 111)

2. have the most comfortable bed.
3. swims the best.
4. have the least time on Thursday.
5. have the fewest children.
6. drives the fastest.

Exercise 5 (p. 111)

Answers will vary.

Exercise 6 (p. 112)

Answers will vary. Some examples are:
1. Brazil is the smallest country.
2. Canada has the longest coastline.
   Brazil has the shortest coastline.

3. China has the most neighbors.
   Canada has the fewest neighbors.
4. China is the most populated country. / China has the largest population. / China has the most people.
   Canada is the least populated country. / Canada has the smallest population. / Canada has the fewest people.

Exercise 7 (p. 113)

It was also the more quiet [~~more~~ quietest], even though it has the most powerful engine of the three. However, the Cheetah was most [the] easiest to handle, and it performed the best at high speeds. At 50 miles per gallon, the Zebra was the most economical of the three models, but it was also the more [most] expensive. All three cars were attractive, but we thought the Onyx was the beautifulest [most beautiful]. Overall, we agreed that the most good [best] buy is probably the Onyx 2000.

Exercise 8 (p. 113)

Answers will vary.

See page 153 for Key to Review: Chapters 18–19.

Chapter 20   Gerunds

Exercise 1 (p. 116)

1. line 6:   trying
   line 7:   losing
   line 9:   maintaining
   line 11: Jogging
   line 12: swimming
   line 12: riding
   line 12: playing
   line 15: helping
   line 17: Increasing
   line 21: weightlifting
   line 23: Doing
   line 30: exercising
2. trying

Exercise 2 (p. 117)

2. Skydiving
3. Not eating too many sweets
4. Joining a club
5. Reading to children
6. Walking

Exercise 3 (p. 117)

2. I don't mind leaving early.
3. Min-hee dislikes being late.
4. We are/We're considering getting a new car.
5. Koji has quit smoking.
6. He suggested talking to you.

Exercise 4 (p. 118)

A. 2. about
   3. about
   4. of

5. at/in
6. to
7. of/about
8. of
9. in
10. on

B. Answers will vary.

Exercise 5 (p. 119)

A. 2. d
   3. a
   4. c
   5. h
   6. b
   7. g
   8. e

B. 1. I like swimming, windsurfing, and scuba diving.
      He loves watching old movies.
   2. Because the sign says "No Trespassing."
   3. I do my laundry, and then I go shopping.
   4. Would you mind not talking so loudly?
      Would you mind giving us a ride home?
   5. By turning it upside down.

Exercise 6 (p. 120)

I really enjoyed to read [reading] them, especially "The Secret Diary of Elizabeth." What a great story!

Anyway, I apologize for I didn't write [not writing] back before now. I've been busy moving into my new apartment. It's more expensive than the old one, so I'm thinking about I might get [getting] a roommate. With a roommate, I can have more money to go ski [skiing], and I might even be able to save some money. Of course, the problem is finding someone I can live with. I've gotten used to live [living] alone, and I'm not looking forward to share [sharing] space with someone.

Also, I might look for another job. Writing letters and reports are [is] getting boring. And my boss and I continue not [~~not~~] getting along. I'm interested in move [moving] into a management position if I can find one. I wouldn't even mind to work [working] part–time for awhile.

So when are you going to come and see my new apartment? You can stay here—if you don't mind to sleep [sleeping] on the sofa! Write back soon and let me know.

Exercise 7 (p. 121)

Answers will vary.

Chapter 21 Infinitives

Exercise 1 (p. 122)

1. b. managed to blow out
   c. helped to make
   d. expect to marry
2. a. in order to protect
   b. to scare
   c. in order to help
   d. to bring
3. a. it's hard to imagine
   b. It was important to be
   c. It was common to put

Exercise 2 (p. 123)

A. 2. to come, too.
3. to get a new car.
4. not to go to college.
5. not to tell anyone.
6. to help us.
7. to babysit the twins.
8. to come.

B. 2. b
3. b
4. a, b
5. a
6. a, b

Exercise 3 (p. 124)

2. it's fun to watch movies at home.
3. it wasn't/isn't easy to find a job.
4. it's too expensive to buy a new one.
5. it's tiring to work all night.
6. it's important to exercise.

Exercise 4 (p. 124)

2. You use a broom (in order) to sweep the floor.
3. You use a washing machine (in order) to wash clothes.
4. You use a trash can (in order) to hold trash.
5. You use a hose (in order) to water the yard.
6. You use a stove (in order) to cook your food.

Exercise 5 (p. 125)

2. . . . going out
3. . . . to going out
4. . . . to go out
5. . . . to going out
6. . . . to go out
7. . . . to go out
8. . . . going out
9. . . . going out
10. . . . to going out

Exercise 6 (p. 125)

2. being
3. to spend

4. meeting
5. to do
6. traveling
7. to live
8. going
9. to have
10. not having
11. to spend
12. to go
13. not to spend

Exercise 7 (p. 126)

2. a
3. a
4. b
5. a
6. b

Exercise 8 (p. 127)

Answers will vary.

Chapter 22 Phrasal Verbs

Exercise 1 (p. 128)

1. B: called...off, aren't getting along, put up with
   C: call...up, 's looking after
   D: ran into, drop by
   E: cut down on, do without

2. **Objects**
   B: called *it* off, put up with *him*
   C: call *Bill* up, 's looking after *the kids*
   D: ran into *Kevin Wu's sister*
   E. cut down on *sugar*, do without *chocolate*

3. **Transitive**
   a. Inseparable: ran into, do without
   b. Three-word: put up with, cut down on
   c. Separable: help out, call off, call up
   Intransitive: get along, drop by

Exercise 2 (p. 129)

2. I called for her.
3. She's dropping it off.
4. I can't do without it.
5. He's reading it over.
6. She looks after him.

Exercise 3 (p. 129)

A. ⊥ 2. drop by

⊤ 3. turn down

⊥ 4. get along

⊤ 5. put on

⊥ 6. sit down

B. Objects: the music, winter boots.
   Please turn the music down.
   It's going to snow today, so put your winter boots on.

Exercise 4 (p. 130)

2. c
3. b
4. c
5. b
6. c

Exercise 5 (p. 130)

Answers will vary. Some examples are:
2. come across
3. go over/read over
4. leave out
5. give back
6. fill out

Exercise 6 (p. 131)

Answers will vary.

Exercise 7 (p. 132)

Answers will vary.

See page 153 for Key to Review: Chapters 20–22.

•

Key to Chapter Reviews

Review: Chapters 1–3 (p. 17)

A.
1. What fish go to heaven?
2. What flowers do you have on your face?
3. When does an old clock die?
4. What words have the most letters?
5. Why does a giraffe have a long neck?
6. When does a doctor get angry?

B.
7. Today is Saturday, and Alex is ~~stay~~ *staying* at home with his family.
8. His mother ~~makes~~ *is making* a chocolate cake in the kitchen.
9. The cake ~~is smelling~~ *smells* great.
10. His father is outside. He ~~washes~~ *'s washing* his car.
11. His sister, Tina, is ~~listen~~ *listening* to music in her bedroom.
12. She is playing it too loud, and Alex ~~is hearing~~ *hears* it in the basement.
13. His sister, Sara, is ~~plays~~ *playing* a video game in the living room.
14. Everybody ~~is seeming~~ *seems* very happy.

C.
15. a
16. b
17. c
18. c
19. a
20. c
21. b
22. b
23. b
24. a
25. c
26. a
27. c
28. a
29. a
30. b

Review: Chapters 4–6 (p. 35)

A.
1. said
2. threw
3. heard
4. flew
5. bought
6. begun
7. sold
8. eaten
9. worn
10. gave
11. fell
12. grown
13. bit
14. lost

B.
15. Not OK
16. OK
17. Not OK
18. OK
19. Not OK
20. Not OK
21. OK

C.
22. c
23. c
24. a
25. c
26. b
27. a
28. c
29. b
30. b

Review: Chapters 7–8 (p. 48)

A.
1. I~~'ll~~ *'m* meeting John after work. / I'll meet John after work.
2. We *'re* not going to Los Angeles this summer.
3. I have an idea: I'~~ll~~ *'ll* pick you up on my way to the airport.
4. Can you turn off the light when you ~~are leaving~~ *leave* the room?
5. Will you ~~being~~ *be* at the party tomorrow?
6. When she ~~will arrive~~ *arrives* home, she will phone her mother.
7. I *'m* going to tell you.
8. This test isn't ~~being~~ easy.

B.
9. b
10. b
11. a
12. a
13. a
14. b
15. a
16. b

C.
17. a
18. c
19. c
20. b
21. a
22. c
23. b
24. b
25. a
26. a
27. b

28. c
29. a
30. c

Review: Chapters 9–11 (p. 65)

A.
1. b
2. a
3. a
4. b
5. a
6. b

B.
7. It might not rain.
8. I wouldn't like to be in his situation.
9. He doesn't have to do it.
10. We'd better not go now.
11. They'd prefer not to wait.
12. She shouldn't leave.
13. He may not come.

C.
14. It's really late. We really should ~~to~~ go home.

15. You don't have ~~got~~ to worry about dinner. Rosa has agreed to cook.

16. Yesterday I ~~could~~ *was able to* run a mile in less than six minutes.

17. They would ~~not~~ rather work late tonight.

18. Where would you like *to* go to college?

19. It's a long way to the station. I'd prefer to drive rather *than* walk.

20. Susan might help~~s~~ with our math homework.

21. When we lived in Africa, we ~~could~~ *were able to/could* see elephants and giraffes.

D.
22. a, b
23. b, c
24. a, c
25. b, c
26. a, c
27. a, b
28. a, c
29. a, b
30. b, c

Review: Chapters 12–13 (p. 77)

A.
1. are
2. neither
3. is
4. would
5. can
6. too
7. so

8. won't
9. does

B.
10. doesn't she
11. was it
12. haven't they
13. do you
14. isn't it
15. don't you
16. were they
17. aren't I
18. have you
19. didn't you
20. could you
21. can't she

C.
22. e
23. c
24. a
25. b
26. d

D.
27. Neither
28. either
29. did
30. too

Review: Chapters 14–15 (p. 89)

A.
1. furniture
2. mail
3. work
4. luck
5. freedom
6. baggage
7. advice
8. gas
9. jewelry
10. money
11. information
12. news

B.
13. The living room is *the* nicest room in the house.

14. It's a small room, and it's next to *the* kitchen.

15. There's a red rug on the floor and *a* large, comfortable sofa to sit on.

16. Across *the* room from the sofa are two armchairs.

17. We have *a* lot of family pictures on the walls.

18. There's ~~the~~ *a* large plant next to the window.

19. The window has ~~the~~ white curtains.

20. I like ~~a~~ *the* living room because I spend time there with my family.

21. Whenever ~~a~~ special shows are on TV, we eat our dinner there.

22. I like to watch TV and eat at ~~a~~ *the* same time.

23. When we have ~~a~~ guests, they sleep on the sofa in the living room.

24. Sometimes I fall asleep in ^*the* living room while watching TV.

C. 25. a, b
26. a, c
27. a, b
28. a, c
29. a, c
30. b, c

Review: Chapters 16–17 (p. 102)

A. 1. The children became terribly ~~exciting~~ *excited* when it started to snow.

2. We can talk later. It's important (nothing).

3. You look hot and ~~tiring~~ *tired*. Do you want to sit down?

4. I like your leather (black) boots. Are they new?

5. Lorraine drives very slow^*ly*.

6. It was ~~so~~ *such* a hot day that we decided to go for a nice, long swim in the lake.

7. You don't exercise (enough) often. You should come to that new gym with me.

8. I have visited (recently) Japan and Korea. It was a wonderful trip.

9. Have you got enough money to buy the computer? It's ~~extreme~~ *extremely* expensive.

10. You need to work ~~more hard~~ *harder* if you want to do well in this class.

B. 11. Could I have some sparkling mineral water?
12. It's a traditional Chinese custom.
13. Perhaps your father will call tonight.
14. The princess was wearing a long black evening dress.
15. He probably doesn't want anything.
16. The officer examined my papers suspiciously.
17. Please don't do anything special for my birthday.
18. We bought a lot of expensive camping equipment.
19. They have some beautiful old Italian furniture.
20. We are definitely going away this summer. / We definitely are going away this summer.

C. 21. b
22. b
23. b
24. b
25. a
26. a
27. b
28. a
29. a
30. b

Review: Chapters 18–19 (p. 114)

A. 1. than
2. richer
3. less
4. least
5. more
6. as
7. most
8. richest

B. 9. more
10. more
11. than
12. does
13. as
14. fewer
15. less
16. least
17. most
18. better
19. more
20. better
21. most

C. 22. Not OK
23. Not OK
24. OK
25. Not OK
26. OK
27. OK
28. Not OK
29. OK
30. OK

Review: Chapters 20–22 (p. 133)

A. 1. a
2. a
3. a
4. a
5. b
6. a
7. b
8. b
9. b
10. a
11. a
12. a
13. a
14. b
15. b

B. 16. a
17. a
18. b
19. b
20. a
21. a

C. 22. out
23. back
24. on
25. up
26. after
27. off
28. with
29. into
30. over